Andrew Davison was
ation he was a scientist. He served his curacy in south east
London and since 2006 has been Tutor in Christian
Doctrine at St Stephen's House in Oxford and junior
chaplain of Merton College, Oxford. He has been appointed
Tutor in Doctrine at Westcott House, Cambridge, from
September 2010. He writes on doctrine, ecclesiology,
philosophical theology and Christian apologetics. He
is the author, with Alison Milbank, of *For the Parish:
A Critique of Fresh Expressions* and editor of *Imaginative
Apologetics: Theology, Philosophy and the Catholic Tradition*
(both SCM Press, 2010). His interests include travel,
architecture, music and dance.

Andrew Nunn was born in Leicester but, since ordination
at Ripon Cathedral in 1983, has lived and worked both
in Leeds and in London. In Leeds he was Vicar of an
inner-city parish, and in Southwark, London, was until
1999 Chaplain to the Bishop, and since then has been
Sub-Dean and Precentor at the cathedral. In addition,
he is Warden of Readers in the diocese, teaches on various
courses and is actively involved in the life of local schools
(he is a foundation governor of St Saviour's & St Olave's
Girls' School). He is also a member of the Church of
England's General Synod and is at present Rector General
of the Society of Catholic Priests. Outside of church, he
enjoys reading, the theatre, art galleries and spending time
with friends over a good meal and a glass of wine.

Toby Wright was born in Oxford and returned there to
read theology at New College. He was then a researcher
for the Westminster Ethical Policy Forum and worked in
a school before undertaking priestly formation at Mirfield.

He served a curacy in Petersfield, and then became Vicar of St John Chrysostom in Peckham, and Area Dean of Camberwell. Since 2009 he has been Team Rector of Witney. He is a national director on the board of Affirming Catholicism and his interests include mission and liturgy. He is married to Sally, who is also ordained, and they have a young son, Caspar. His interests include cooking and following the England rugby squad from the sofa.

LIFT UP YOUR HEARTS

Prayers for Anglicans

Andrew Davison, Andrew Nunn
and Toby Wright

First published in Great Britain in 2010

Society for Promoting Christian Knowledge
36 Causton Street
London SW1P 4ST
www.spckpublishing.co.uk

British Library Cataloguing-in-Publication Data
A catalogue record for this book is available from the British Library

ISBN 978–0–281–06149–5

1 3 5 7 9 10 8 6 4 2

Typeset by Graphicraft Ltd, Hong Kong
Printed in Great Britain by the MPG Books Group

Produced on paper from sustainable forests

*To the glory of God and in thanksgiving for
the Anglican tradition*

Prayer, the Church's banquet, Angels' age.
   God's breath in man returning to his birth,
   The soul in paraphrase, heart in pilgrimage,
The Christian plummet sounding heaven and earth;
Engine against th' Almighty, sinners' tower,
   Reversèd thunder, Christ-side-piercing spear,
   The six-days' world transposing in an hour,
A kind of tune, which all things hear and fear;
Softness, and peace, and joy, and love, and bliss.
   Exalted Manna, gladness of the best,
   Heaven in ordinary, man well drest,
The Milky Way, the bird of Paradise,
   Church-bells beyond the stars heard, the soul's blood,
   The land of spices; something understood.

              (George Herbert, 1593–1633)

Contents

Foreword   ix

Introduction   xi

1 Praising God together   1

2 Confession and forgiveness   14

3 Prayer and silence   22

4 Praying with the word of God   29

5 Praying for the world   41

6 Peace and reconciliation   68

7 Prayers at meals   77

8 Thanksgiving and the Holy Spirit   82

9 Praying the Our Father   91

10 Communion and the Sacrament   98

11 Blessing and the world; work and
    the day's ending   106

Appendix: Prayers and devotions   116

Sources and acknowledgements   133

Suggestions for further reading   142

Index   144

Foreword

————•◦•————

I can't be the only priest who has sat at the deathbeds of elderly and much loved fellow pilgrims and marvelled at their faith, but has also been humbled by the prayers they know by heart, and by how these prayers sustained them in their final journeys. I suppose after a lifetime of church-going it is not unusual to know the main prayers of the liturgy by heart, but Christians of a previous generation seemed to know so much more.

I remember a lady to whom I regularly took Holy Communion at home in her little South London council flat; she not only knew all the prayers she was supposed to say, she knew mine as well, and would join in the collects, word perfect, week by week. I can only conclude that learning prayers by heart, that owning and loving a book of prayers, was part of a spiritual tradition that has been neglected in our age. We have tended to think that to be authentic, heartfelt prayer must be in our own words, spontaneous and inspired. But this can't be right. Jesus himself taught his disciples to pray by giving them the words to say. And they learnt these words and faithfully passed them on and they have become the bedrock of all praying. And as Anglicans we believe it is through the words of our prayer that we learn and define our faith. Therefore the words are never just 'our words', they are also the words of the Church, and they are hallowed, inten-sified and refined by their very repetition, and by their becoming part of the fabric of this living tradition that is our catholic faith. Moreover, there are times when all of us feel barren, bereft, uninspired and distant from God.

It is at precisely these times that we need the resource of someone else's words, and we need to be part of a faith that is not just about us, and is not just dependent on our own feelings or understanding.

This is where a book of prayers is so valuable. It is not just a help, it is a foothold above the abyss; it is an oasis in the desert; it is a lifebelt thrown to a drowning man. I can pray the prayers of the Church. I can unite my prayers with the prayer of others. The voice of my prayer, however faltering or frail, can be part of the great offering of prayer which is the vocation of the Church, uniting its voice to the voice of heaven. That is what it means to lift up your hearts: united with others, with heaven itself, we are lifting them to God.

This, then, is a book we need. Taking its shape and pattern from the Eucharist, which is the centre of the Church's offering of worship, this book gives prayers and reflections about prayer as resources for and encouragement to Christian people in their spiritual journey. The prayers lead us through the Eucharist, but they also lead us through life, to that day which will be our last day and where we will offer a last prayer. So while there are plenty of books of prayers for clergy, and in the past there have been quite a lot like this one for lay people, a new one for today's Church is a timely reminder that though we may often find ourselves alone in prayer, this is never actually the case. We are surrounded by the prayers of others and we are supplied by a tradition we can make our own.

Stephen Cottrell
Bishop of Chelmsford

Introduction

The disciples gathered around Jesus and said to him, 'Lord, teach us to pray' (Luke 11.1). That desire to pray is a deep and natural one for all Christians. None of us think of ourselves as particularly good at prayer, even those who have devoted their lives to it. We each think that we could pray better than we do but we want someone to teach us, or someone to give us the resources from which to build up our prayer and devotional life. It is responding to this desire that lies behind this book, which contains not just prayers but reflections on what we are doing when we pray.

The Eucharist at the heart

For the vast majority of Anglicans their experience of the Church at prayer is in the Eucharist. This is particularly the case for catholic Anglicans for whom the Mass is at the heart of their life and for whom receiving communion on a weekly or even daily basis is how their relationship with God is lived out.

Because the Eucharist is so central to our lives this book takes its structure from that service. Anyone familiar with the shape of the Eucharist in *Common Worship* will be able to follow the way in which this book has been prepared. Each chapter, and the prayers that it contains, follows the pattern of entering into church, confessing our sins, hearing and responding to the word of God, preparing the altar, receiving communion and leaving the gathering. The selection of prayers is intended to deepen our own devotion at each part of the liturgy, but not just when we are in church. Some prayers will be useful when we are at worship with others, but other prayers will be for our own devotions at other times. The Appendix contains other material which does not fit neatly into the structure of the Mass but which is important for the undergirding of our spiritual lives as catholic Anglicans.

A heritage of prayer

As Anglicans we have a rich heritage of prayer on which to draw and this book looks to that inheritance. As catholics there is the western tradition of which we are part, informed by the Orthodox tradition from the East. As members of a worldwide communion there is much that we are learning from prayer traditions in other places. In addition we have a concept of a living and evolving liturgy that takes seriously the issues of the day and the lives we live. In traditional and con-temporary prayers this book seeks to bring together all these strands.

An aspect of this heritage is memorizing some of the great prayers which help to make us who we are. Some of the collects from the Book of Common Prayer, prayers from *Common Worship* that we use regularly and prayers by some of the saints should be part of what we carry with us in our memory. When our own words fail us then the familiar and remembered words from our heritage can give us a voice.

A wealth of theology

An aspect of our life that is particularly important for Anglicans is that it is in the liturgy of the Church that we can find our doctrine. If Anglicans are asked, 'What do you believe?', they should respond by taking the enquirer to church. The faith of the Church is lived out and understood in worship. We learn our theology and we deepen our understanding of God when we pray. This book is therefore not just a selection of prayers but an exercise in theology. People who pray are people who do theology, who know God.

The fact that many of the prayers in this book are drawn from the two thousand years of tradition of which we are inheritors means that the language used reflects theological understanding and positions of other times as well as other forms of language in use. Where it has been felt that traditional language is important for the depth of the prayer the text has not been rendered into modern English. Where traditional language would obscure the meaning then it has been sensitively adapted. For the same reason God is often referred to as 'he' and, whereas there is now good reason to look for ways of addressing and thinking about God that are not gender-specific, we have consciously left 'male language' referring to God without wanting to suggest that this is the way we would always think about God.

Using the book

This book is intended to be useful, not another book for the shelf but to accompany us in our journey. King Henry VIII's prayer book in the British Library shows his comments and own prayers in the margins. The book really became his prayer book and reflects his own spirituality and theological thinking. Add your own comments in the margins, highlight a prayer you will use regularly, add extra ribbons and use the blank page at the back of the book to supplement this volume with other prayers that you come across and find useful. Make this your working journal of prayer as you lift up your heart, day by day, to God.

The Church's banquet

When we pray we learn to pray; as we pray we enter into that rich experience of prayer which George Herbert describes in his poem at the front of this book, in a series of metaphors that seek to describe this 'banquet' of riches.

Affirming Catholicism and the Society of Catholic Priests, who have sponsored this prayer book, are committed to the catholic tradition of the Church of which we are part. 'Lift up your hearts,' says the priest from the altar. 'We lift them to the Lord,' we respond. As we pray that is exactly what we do.

1

Praising God together

————◆•◆•◆————

The experience of going to church begins before we actually arrive at the place where the service will be celebrated. There are things that we should do in order to get ourselves ready to worship God. Every Sunday is in fact a mini-Easter, a celebration of the Lord's Resurrection, the first day of the week and a time for new beginnings. Sunday is also the time when the Christian community gathers and together we offer worship to God and serve one another in his name.

Beginning any day is important, not just beginning Sunday in a way that will help us celebrate properly the amazing acts of God. When we wake from sleep we want to give thanks for the rest we have enjoyed and we anticipate all that the day will hold. We then need to prepare ourselves for the things that we know we will be doing and the things that will happen for which we cannot be prepared.

In this chapter you will find material to begin the day with acts of praise and prayers that will help us enter the day with joy. There are also prayers to offer for all those who are going to be involved in ministry in any way – not just the clergy and other ministers, but the welcomers and coffee makers, the bell-ringers and the servers.

As we celebrate the resurrection of Jesus we are also reminded that we have shared in his resurrection through our baptism, and as we come to church it is a good opportunity to remember our own baptism and those who have guided us in the faith, not least our godparents. The life that Jesus gives us is an abundant life and it is that which we wake to celebrate.

Prayers of praise

May the Lord be blessed for ever for the great gifts that he has continually heaped upon me, and may all that he has created praise him. Amen.

(St Teresa of Avila, 1515–82)

You are holy, Lord, the only God
and your deeds are wonderful.
You are strong, you are great.
You are the Most High, you are almighty.
You Holy Father, are King of heaven and earth.
You are Three and One, Lord God, all good.
You are Good, all Good, supreme Good,
Lord God, living and true.
You are love, you are wisdom.
You are humility, you are endurance.
You are rest, you are peace.
You are joy and gladness.
You are justice and moderation.
You are all our riches and you suffice for us.
You are beauty, you are gentleness.
You are our protector,
you are our guardian and defender.
You are courage, you are our haven and our hope.
You are our faith, our great consolation.
You are our eternal life, great and wonderful Lord,
God almighty, merciful Saviour.

(St Francis of Assisi, *c.* 1182–1226, 'The Praises of God')

The Te Deum

We praise you, O God,
we acclaim you as the Lord;
all creation worships you,

the Father everlasting.
To you all angels, all the powers of heaven,
the cherubim and seraphim, sing in endless praise:
Holy, holy, holy Lord, God of power and might,
heaven and earth are full of your glory.
The glorious company of apostles praise you.
The noble fellowship of prophets praise you.
The white-robed army of martyrs praise you.
Throughout the world the holy Church acclaims you:
Father, of majesty unbounded,
your true and only Son, worthy of all praise,
the Holy Spirit, advocate and guide.
You, Christ, are the King of glory,
the eternal Son of the Father.
When you took our flesh to set us free
you humbly chose the Virgin's womb.
You overcame the sting of death
and opened the kingdom of heaven to all believers.
You are seated at God's right hand in glory.
We believe that you will come and be our judge.
Come then, Lord, and help your people,
bought with the price of your own blood,
and bring us with your saints
to glory everlasting.

The canticle may end here.

Save your people, Lord, and bless your inheritance.
Govern and uphold them now and always.
Day by day we bless you.
We praise your name for ever.
Keep us today, Lord, from all sin.
Have mercy on us, Lord, have mercy.
Lord, show us your love and mercy,
for we have put our trust in you.
In you, Lord, is our hope:
let us never be put to shame.

(*Common Worship: Daily Prayer*)

An acclamation of praise

Worthy of praise from every mouth,
of confession from every tongue,
of worship from every creature,
is your Glorious Name,
O Father, Son, and Holy Spirit:
you created the world with your imprint
and by your compassion you saved it.

To your majesty, O God,
ten thousand times ten thousand
bow down and adore,
singing and praising without ceasing,
and saying Holy, Holy, Holy,
Lord God of hosts;
Heaven and earth are full of your praises;
Hosanna in the highest.

(Nestorian Liturgy)*

Dedication at the start of the day

We give you hearty thanks
for the rest of the past night
and for the gift of a new day,
with its opportunities for pleasing you.
Grant that we may so pass its hours
in the perfect freedom of your service,
that at eventide we may again give thanks unto you;
through Jesus Christ our Lord. Amen.

(Eastern Church Liturgy Daybreak Office)*

O Lord, thou knowest how busy I must be this day: if I
forget thee, do not thou forget me; for Christ's sake. Amen.

(General Lord Astley, before the Battle of Edgehill, 1642)

My life is an instant,
An hour which passes by;

My life is a moment
Which I have no power to stay.
You know, O my God,
That to love you here on earth
I have only today.
(St Thérèse of Lisieux, 1873–97)

O Lord Christ, help us to maintain ourselves in simplicity and in joy, the joy of the merciful, the joy of brotherly love. Grant that, renouncing henceforth all thought of looking back, and joyful with infinite gratitude, we may never fear to precede the dawn to praise and bless and sing to Christ our Lord.
(Based on the Rule of Taizé)

My Father, I abandon myself to you. Do with me as you will. Whatever you may do with me, I thank you. I am prepared for anything, I accept everything. Provided your will is fulfilled in me and in all creatures I ask for nothing more, my God. I place my soul in your hands. I give it to you, my God, with all the love of my heart because I love you.
(Blessed Charles de Foucauld, 1858–1916)

O God, forasmuch as without thee we are not able to please thee; Mercifully grant, that thy Holy Spirit may in all things direct and rule our hearts; through Jesus Christ our Lord. Amen.   (Book of Common Prayer)

Teach us, Good Lord,
to serve you as you deserve,
to give and not to count the cost,
to fight and not to heed the wounds,
to toil and not to seek for rest,
to labour and not to ask for any reward,
save that of knowing that we do your will,
through Jesus Christ our Lord. Amen.
(St Ignatius of Loyola, 1491–1556)

Keep us safe in soul and body,
make us a blessing
to our friends and family,
and help us,
in everything we do,
to bear ourselves in such a way
as to further your kingdom,
through Jesus Christ
your Son our Saviour. Amen.   (James Ferguson)

At the beginning of work

O God, who hast ordained that whatever is to be desired
should be sought by labour, and who, by thy blessing,
bringest honest labour to good effect, look with mercy
upon my studies and endeavours. Grant me, O Lord,
to design only what is lawful and right; and afford me
calmness of mind and steadiness of purpose, that I may
so do thy will in this short life as to obtain happiness in
the world to come.   (Samuel Johnson, 1709–84)

Forth in thy Name, O Lord, I go,
My daily labour to pursue;
Thee, only thee, resolved to know
In all I think or speak or do.

The task thy wisdom hath assigned,
O let me cheerfully fulfil,
In all my works thy presence find,
And prove thy good and perfect will.
          (Charles Wesley, 1707–88)

O Lord Jesus Christ,
Only Son of your Eternal Father,
You said with your most pure lips:
Without me you can do nothing.
O Lord, my Lord,
With faith I embrace in my heart and soul

the words you have spoken.
Help me, a sinner,
To accomplish the task
That I begin for your sake,
In the Name of the Father,
and of the Son,
and of the Holy Spirit. Amen.
(Eastern Orthodox prayer before beginning any action)

Teach me, my God and King,
In all things thee to see,
And what I do in anything
To do it as for thee.   (George Herbert, 1593–1633)

Preparation for worship

O Lord our God,
grant us grace to desire you with our whole heart:
that desiring you,
we may seek and find you;
and finding you we may love you;
and loving you we may hate those sins
from which you have redeemed us;
for the sake of Jesus Christ. Amen.
(St Anselm, 1033–1109)

On entering or passing a church where the Blessed Sacrament is reserved

We adore you,
most holy Lord Jesus Christ,
here, and in all your churches
throughout the world;
and we bless you,
because, by your holy cross,
you have redeemed the world. Amen.
(An ancient prayer from the Liturgy
for Holy Thursday, quoted by ·
St Francis of Assisi, *c.* 1182–1226)

The Collect for Purity

Almighty God, unto whom all hearts be open, all desires known, and from whom no secrets are hid: Cleanse the thoughts of our hearts by the inspiration of thy Holy Spirit, that we may perfectly love thee, and worthily magnify thy holy Name; through Christ our Lord. Amen.

(Book of Common Prayer)

A prayer before worship

Divine Saviour,
we come to your sacred table
to nourish ourselves, not with bread but with yourself,
true Bread of eternal life.
Help us daily to make a good and perfect meal
of this divine food.
Let us be continually refreshed
by the perfume of your kindness and goodness.
May the Holy Spirit fill us with his love.
Meanwhile, let us prepare a place for this holy food
by emptying our hearts. Amen.

(St Francis de Sales, 1567–1622)

Preparing for ministry

The belfry prayer

We beseech thee, O Heavenly Father,
to pour thy grace into the hearts
of those who work for Thee
in ringing the bells of the Church.
Grant that we may never forget
the sacredness of Thy House,
nor profane it by thoughtlessness or irreverence,
but make us ever mindful that when we ring the bells,
we ring for Thy honour and glory;
through Jesus Christ our Lord.

(St Stephen's Church, Canterbury)*

The altar servers' prayer

Loving Father, creator of the universe,
you call your people to worship,
to be with you and with one another
    at the Eucharist.
I thank you for having called me
to assist others in their prayer to you.
May I be worthy of the trust placed in me
and through my example and service
bring others closer to you.
I ask this in the name of Jesus Christ,
who is Lord for ever and ever. Amen.   (Anonymous)

The choristers' prayer

Bless, O Lord, us thy servants,
who minister in thy temple.
Grant that what we sing with our lips,
we may believe in our hearts,
and what we believe in our hearts,
we may show forth in our lives.
Through Jesus Christ our Lord. Amen.
                (RSCM Choristers' Prayer)

The welcomers' prayer

Lord, I would rather be a doorkeeper in your house
than dwell in the tents of the ungodly.
Bless my ministry today
that I may welcome all who come into your house,
for I know that in welcoming them
I welcome you,
both host and guest at every table. Amen.   (AN)

The lectors' prayer

Praise to you, Lord God,
king of the universe,
and all glory to your name.

I praise you and thank you for calling me
to proclaim your word to your beloved people.
Open the hearts of all who worship with us,
so that they may hear your voice when I read.
Let nothing in my life or manner
   disturb your people
or close their hearts to the action of your Spirit.
Cleanse my heart and mind,
and open my lips so that I may proclaim your glory.
All praise to you, heavenly Father,
through the Lord Jesus in the Holy Spirit,
now and for ever. Amen.   (Anonymous)

The intercessors' prayer

Lord Jesus,
you told us to ask for anything in your name.
Inspire me as I prepare to bring before you
the needs and prayers of my sisters and brothers.
May I so pray,
that they may find both strength and comfort
and together we may bring to you
the world, the church and your people. Amen.
      (Anonymous)

The eucharistic ministers' prayer

Jesus, bless these hands you have chosen as your tools.
Jesus, always keep us aware
and in awe of our sacred mission.
Jesus, make us worthy of this great ministry
we have humbly accepted.
Jesus, send us out into the world
to distribute your love. Amen.   (Anonymous)

The coffee makers' prayer

Lord Jesus, you loved to share a meal with your friends
and provided wine at a wedding
to make the party whole.

Thank you for giving me the privilege
of serving your family today,
and may the hospitality that we offer after church
reflect the hospitality of your table
where we have gathered
to eat and drink in fellowship with you. Amen.   (AN)

A prayer for your priest(s)

Jesus Christ, our great high priest,
bless those who minister to us
and especially the priest(s) in our parish.
Give to them wisdom and insight,
compassion and humility,
that in all they do and say
they may make you known
and your kingdom real. Amen.   (AN)

Remembering our baptism

O God,
who by the Baptism of your only Son
sanctified the streams of water;
grant that we who are born again
of water and the Spirit
may gain an entrance into eternal joys;
through the same Jesus Christ our Lord. Amen.
                    (Gregorian, as edited by Pamelius)*

A prayer on the anniversary of baptism

Loving God
on this day I was born again
and made one with you through baptism.
I thank you for my fellowship in your universal Church.
Keep me faithful to my baptism
and bring me at the last to my eternal home
where I can worship you with the saints for ever. Amen.
                    (AN)

A prayer for godchildren

Lord Jesus, you called the children to you
And blessed them.
Bless my godchild(ren) *N. & N.*
Fill *them* with an ever deepening knowledge of you,
Guide *their* steps today
And keep *them* in safety
For your love's sake. Amen.   (AN)

A prayer for our godparents

God and Father of us all,
I pray for those who accepted the responsibility
to serve as my godparents.
Help them by your grace to fulfil their duties
and keep them faithful in prayer;
that under their care and guidance
I may grow into the person you want me to be,
in the faith of Jesus Christ
and in the fellowship of the Church. Amen.
                    (Frank Colquhoun, *New Parish Prayers*)

Does prayer change anything?

Do things turn out differently because we pray? Prayer certainly changes the world in one obvious way: it makes it a world in which people pray. This is a better sort of world, one where we are more honest about our needs and our status as God's creatures. Whatever else we might say, it is right and fitting that we should commend ourselves and others into God's care.

God wishes to draw us into his work. He gives us good things whether we pray or not, but when we do pray he shares his work with us. He gives us, in answer to prayer, what he could have given without. In this way, intercessory prayer changes things by making us into God's co-workers.

Finally, we need also to say that prayer does influence the course of the events themselves. This is the message of the Bible and of the Christian tradition. We pray to God who is Lord of all things, the creator and ruler of space and time. 'If you then, who are evil, know how to give good gifts to your children, how much more will your Father in heaven give good things to those who ask him!' (Matthew 7.11).

2

Confession and forgiveness

After being greeted at the beginning of the Eucharist we move almost instantaneously into an invitation to recall and confess our sins. Other traditions sometimes place this later in the service so that confession comes in response to the reading and consideration of God's word. However, for the majority of catholic Christians this is where we begin. The rationale is that when we approach God in worship we are naturally mindful of what holds us back from perfect union with the Trinity of love.

We are normally not given very long to recall our sins when we get to church. We may be able to remember something that we have said or done on the way to church – but not necessarily something we did a few days ago; we may remember some major sin, but what about all those less important, niggling sins?

This is where preparing for coming to the Eucharist becomes really important. It isn't easy to do but it is a habit of prayer and preparation well worth developing, that of spending time before coming to church examining our conscience and preparing ourselves to make a good and true confession of all our sins. It is not easy because it means seeing ourselves as God sees us, knowing ourselves as God knows us.

You will find here resources and prayers to help you to do this preparation but more important than any prayer is a willingness to be honest and open with God and with ourselves and to receive that generous and gracious forgiveness, the embrace of the father of the prodigal, that always awaits us.

Examination of conscience

See the appendix for an order for sacramental confession.

An act of contrition

My God, for love of you
I desire to hate and forsake all sins
by which I have ever displeased you;
and I resolve by the help of your grace
to commit them no more;
and to avoid all opportunities of sin.
Help me to do this,
through Jesus Christ our Lord. Amen.
    (*Common Worship: Christian Initiation*)

Grant Lord, that I may not, for one moment, admit willingly into my soul any thought contrary to thy love.
    (E. B. Pusey, 1800–82)

Prayers of penitence

Preparation

I will get up and go to my father, and I will say to him, 'Father, I have sinned against heaven and before you.'
    (Luke 15.18)

Teach us, O Lord,
to be penitent for our own sins,
rather than severe to others;
and plant in our hearts such forbearance towards all,
such gentleness and forgiveness,

that we, recompensing no one evil for evil,
may in the strength of your Son
overcome evil with good.

(James Ferguson)*

Prayers for pardon

Grant, we beseech thee, merciful Lord, to thy faithful people
pardon and peace; that they may be cleansed from all their
sins and serve thee with a quiet mind; through Jesus Christ
our Lord. Amen. (Book of Common Prayer)

Almighty God,
long-suffering and of great goodness;
I confess to you, I confess with my whole heart,
my neglect and forgetfulness of your
commandments,
my wrong doing, thinking, and speaking;
the hurts I have done to others,
and the good I have left undone.

O God, forgive me, for I have sinned against you;
and raise me to newness of life;
through Jesus Christ our Lord. Amen.
(Eric Milner-White, 1884–1963)

Lord, by this sweet and saving Sign,
Defend us from our foes and thine.
Jesu, by thy wounded feet,
Direct our path aright:
Jesu, by thy nailed hands,
Move ours to deeds of love:
Jesu, by thy pierced side,
Cleanse our desires:
Jesu, by thy crown of thorns,
Annihilate our pride:
Jesu, by thy silence,
Shame our complaints:

Jesu, by thy parched lips,
Curb our cruel speech:
Jesu, by thy closing eyes,
Look on our sin no more:
Jesu, by thy broken heart,
Knit ours to thee.
Yea, by this sweet and saving Sign,
Lord, draw us to our peace and thine.
> (*Cuddesdon Office Book*, 1940 – the first line
> refers to the Holy Cross)

Holy God,
Holy and mighty,
Holy and immortal:
Have mercy on us.
> (The Eastern Orthodox 'Trisagion')

Lord Jesus Christ, Son of God, have mercy on me, a
sinner. (The Jesus Prayer)

We [sinners] beseech thee to hear us, good Lord; That it
may please thee to give us true repentance; to forgive
us all our sins, negligences, and ignorances; and to endue
us with the grace of thy Holy Spirit, to amend our lives
according to thy Holy Word.
> (Adapted from the Litany, Book of Common Prayer)

A litany of penitence

Christ our Saviour is our advocate with the Father:
with humble hearts let us ask him to forgive us our sins
and cleanse us from every stain.

You were sent with good news for the poor
and healing for the contrite.
Lord, be merciful to me, a sinner.
You came to call sinners, not the righteous.
Lord, be merciful to me, a sinner.

You forgave the many sins of the woman who showed
  you great love.
Lord, be merciful to me, a sinner.
You did not shun the company of outcasts and sinners.
Lord, be merciful to me, a sinner.
You carried back to the fold the sheep that had strayed.
Lord, be merciful to me, a sinner.
You did not condemn the woman taken in adultery,
but said, 'Go and sin no more.'
Lord, be merciful to me, a sinner.
You called Zacchaeus to repentance and a new life.
Lord, be merciful to me, a sinner.
You promised Paradise to the repentant thief.
Lord, be merciful to me, a sinner.
You are always interceding for us
at the right hand of the Father.
Lord, be merciful to me, a sinner.

(Common Worship: Christian Initiation)

Resolution of amendment

Lord, I will strive earnestly to do what is good and right.
I have laid my sins at the foot of your cross;
now I desire not to fall back into my old ways.
If I abide in you, I shall not sin.
Therefore help me by your grace
to dwell in your Spirit
and to trust in your love,
That I may live in perfect harmony with you
all the days of my life. Amen.

(Percy Dearmer, 1867–1936)*

Prayer of forgiveness

O Lord, remember not only
the men and women of good will,
but also those of ill will.
But do not remember all the suffering
they have inflicted on us;

remember the fruits we have bought,
thanks to this suffering –
our comradeship, our loyalty, our humility,
our courage, our generosity,
the greatness of heart which has grown out of all this,
and when they come to judgement
let all the fruits which we have borne
be their forgiveness.
(Prayer written by an unknown prisoner in Ravensbruck
concentration camp and left by the body of a dead child)

Prayer after making your confession

Merciful Lord,
with a pure heart
I thank you for taking away my sins.
Let your Holy Spirit guide my life
so that my soul may bear the fruit
of love, joy, peace, patience,
kindness, goodness, trustfulness,
gentleness, and self-control.
Renew my desire to be
your faithful friend and servant,
increase my loving dependence on you,
and grant me that joy and peace of heart
which comes from doing your holy will,
through Christ our Lord. Amen.
(*St Benedict's Prayer Book*)

O Lord,
grant us grace
never to tamper with the truth,
never to dally with temptation,
never to spare anything that is a snare to us,
never to sell our soul,
though in exchange
we should gain the whole world.
(Christina Rossetti, 1830–94)

Bless the Lord, O my soul,
and all that is within me bless his holy name.
Bless the Lord, O my soul,
and forget not all his benefits;
Who forgives all your sins
and heals all your infirmities;
Who redeems your life from the Pit
and crowns you with faithful love and compassion;
Who satisfies you with good things,
so that your youth is renewed like an eagle's.
The Lord executes righteousness
and judgement for all who are oppressed.
He has not dealt with us according to our sins,
nor rewarded us according to our wickedness.
For as the heavens are high above the earth,
so great is his mercy upon those who fear him.
As far as the east is from the west,
so far has he set our sins from us.
As a father has compassion on his children,
so is the Lord merciful towards those who fear him.
Glory to the Father, and to the Son
and to the Holy Spirit;
as it was in the beginning is now
and shall be for ever. Amen.

(*Common Worship*, from Psalm 103)

Praying with the body

A human being is not a soul trapped in a body. We are thoroughly bodily people. We bring our whole self – including our bodies – into our encounter with God in prayer. We pray not only with intellect, memory and will but also with limbs and senses, mouths and ears.

In the Old Testament we find people praying by lifting up their hands, by bowing before God and by going on pilgrimage journeys. As Christians, we pray in all of these ways. We also kneel in penitence, stand in joy, bend the knee in reverence – a gesture called genuflection – and make the sign of the cross on our bodies to honour Christ. If this is unfamiliar, we can ask our clergy, or other Christians who have been praying for a long time, to explain how to do them.

These actions involve us in the liturgy and make it our own prayer too. Nor should we forget that our bodies are involved in prayer because we need to get out of bed and make it to church. Finally, having prayed with the body, we help to answer our prayer with the body, by working to make the world a kinder and more just place, where people know God and love him.

3

Prayer and silence

———•◆•———

At the beginning of the Liturgy of the Word in the Eucharist the president says 'Let us pray' and then there is a time of silence. That silence is an important time for us to offer to God our own intention for that celebration, our own reason for being at that particular celebration. Using silence during the Eucharist is really important, but so is using silent moments at any time of the day. As the story about Elijah shows, it is in the silence and not in the earthquake that God is encountered.

Following the silence the president then collects together our individual prayers in a corporate collect. During the major seasons of the year the collects point to elements of what we are celebrating. During the half of the year that is called 'ordinary time', the Trinity season, the prayers are of a more general character.

In this chapter you will find a selection of wonderful collects that are drawn from the liturgies of the Church of England. Some are in traditional language, some in a contemporary style. The language is incidental – the power of the collect is in what it says. Many of these prayers are worth committing to memory, so that you have them to hand whenever you need words to pray and words simply fail you. These collects are our treasure-house of prayer and as good householders we bring out from our store things old and things new.

Prayer in silence

O Lord, the Scripture says, 'There is a time for silence and a time for speech.' Saviour, teach me the silence of humility, the silence of wisdom, the silence of love, the silence of perfection, the silence that speaks without words, the silence of faith. Lord teach me to silence my own heart that I may listen to the gentle movement of the Holy Spirit within me and sense the depths which are of God.

(Source unknown, sixteenth century)

In silence
To be there before you
Lord, that's all.
To shut the eyes of my body,
To shut the eyes of my soul,
And to be still and silent,
To expose myself to you who are there,
exposed to me.

To be there before you, the Eternal Presence.
I am willing to feel nothing, Lord,
to see nothing, to hear nothing.

Empty of all ideas, of all images,
In the darkness.
Here I am, simply
To meet you without obstacles,
In the silence of faith,
Before you, Lord.
(Michel Quoist, 1921–97, *Prayers of Life*)

O Jesus, Son of God,
who wast silent before Pilate,
do not let us wag our tongues
without thinking of what we are to say
and of how to say it.   (Anonymous Irish)

O God,
make us children of quietness
and heirs of peace.

    (Clement of Rome, first century)

Praying in silence

When we pray in silence we enter into the deepest meaning of prayer. We stand before God in love and gratitude, a creature before the Creator.

Silent prayer is important but it can also be difficult. Quiet is disconcerting for contemporary people, and the lack of activity even more so. Most of us are continually busy, so any minutes we give over to silence can seem very costly. This is no bad thing: silent prayer is a sacrifice of praise, and an indication that we are serious about praying. Likely as not, it will also be good for us psychologically, as addiction to activity is not healthy. Although we do not want to reduce prayer to its benefits for body and mind, we should not be ashamed of them either.

When we pray in silence, distractions are bound to enter into our thoughts. A good way to react is to turn every 'distraction' into a matter for prayer.

Prayer in silence is also a good way to end a period of Bible study or spiritual reading. We may be left with one idea or phrase that we want to turn over in our minds.

Collects

This is just a selection of the collects that can be found in the Book of Common Prayer, in *Common Worship* and elsewhere. Remembering collects is a useful way of filling your 'knapsack' of prayer. They can be a resource at any time and in any situation where words fail you.

From the Book of Common Prayer 1662

Almighty God, give us grace that we may cast away the works of darkness, and put upon us the armour of light, now in the time of this mortal life, in which thy Son Jesus Christ came to visit us in great humility; that in the last day, when he shall come again in his glorious Majesty, to judge both the quick and the dead, we may rise to the life immortal; through him who liveth and reigneth with thee and the Holy Ghost, now and ever. Amen.

(Collect for Advent Sunday,
prayed daily throughout the season)

Almighty and everlasting God, who hatest nothing that thou hast made, and dost forgive the sins of all them that are penitent: Create and make in us new and contrite hearts, that we worthily lamenting our sins, and acknowledging our wretchedness, may obtain of thee, the God of all mercy, perfect remission and forgiveness; through Jesus Christ our Lord. Amen.

(Collect for Ash Wednesday,
prayed daily throughout the season)

O Lord, we beseech thee mercifully to receive the prayers of thy people which call upon thee; and grant that they may both perceive and know what things they ought to do, and also may have grace and power faithfully to fulfil the same; through Jesus Christ our Lord. Amen.

(Collect for the First Sunday after Epiphany)

O God, who knowest us to be set in the midst of so many and great dangers, that by reason of the frailty of our nature we cannot always stand upright: Grant to us such strength and protection, as may support us in all dangers, and carry us through all temptations; through Jesus Christ our Lord. Amen.

(Collect for the Fourth Sunday after Epiphany)

O Almighty God, who alone canst order the unruly wills and affections of sinful men; Grant unto thy people, that they may love the thing which thou commandest, and desire that which thou dost promise; that so, among the sundry and manifold changes of the world, our hearts may surely there be fixed, where true joys are to be found; through Jesus Christ our Lord. Amen.

(Collect for the Fourth Sunday after Easter)

O God, the protector of all that trust in thee, without whom nothing is strong, nothing is holy: Increase and multiply upon us thy mercy; that, thou being our ruler and guide, we may so pass through things temporal, that we finally lose not the things eternal: Grant this, O heavenly Father, for Jesus Christ's sake our Lord. Amen.

(Collect for the Fourth Sunday after Trinity)

Almighty and everlasting God, who art always more ready to hear than we to pray, and art wont to give more than either we desire or deserve: Pour down upon us the abundance of thy mercy; forgiving us those things whereof our conscience is afraid, and giving us those good things which we are not worthy to ask, but through the merits and mediation of Jesus Christ, thy Son, our Lord. Amen.

(Collect for the Twelfth Sunday after Trinity)

Prevent us, O Lord, in all our doings, with thy most gracious favour, and further us with thy continual help; that in all our works begun, continued, and ended in thee, we may glorify thy holy Name, and finally by thy mercy obtain everlasting life; through Jesus Christ our Lord. Amen.

(Collect to be said after the Offertory, when there is no Communion; and on various other occasions)

From *Common Worship*

Almighty God,
whose most dear Son went not up to joy
   but first he suffered pain,
and entered not into glory before he was crucified:
mercifully grant that we, walking in the way of the cross,
may find it none other than the way of life and peace;
through Jesus Christ your Son our Lord,
who is alive and reigns with you,
in the unity of the Holy Spirit,
one God, now and for ever. Amen.
                 (Collect for the Third Sunday of Lent)

O God, whose beauty is beyond our imagining
and whose power we cannot comprehend:
show us your glory as far as we can grasp it,
and shield us from knowing more than we can bear
until we may look upon you without fear;
through Jesus Christ our Saviour. Amen.
                 (Post Communion for the Third Sunday
                            after Trinity)

From *Common Worship: Additional Collects*

Eternal Lord,
our beginning and our end:
bring us with the whole creation
to your glory, hidden through past ages
and made known
in Jesus Christ our Lord. Amen.
       (Collect for the Second Sunday after Epiphany)

Almighty God,
give us reverence for all creation
and respect for every person,
that we may mirror your likeness
in Jesus Christ our Lord. Amen.
       (Collect for the Second Sunday before Lent)

Creator God,
you made us all in your image:
may we discern you in all that we see,
and serve you in all that we do;
through Jesus Christ our Lord. Amen.
    (Collect for the Sixth Sunday after Trinity)

Faithful Lord,
whose steadfast love never ceases
and whose mercies never come to an end:
grant us the grace to trust you
and to receive the gifts of your love,
new every morning,
in Jesus Christ our Lord. Amen.
    (Collect for the Nineteenth Sunday after Trinity)

4

Praying with the word of God

In the evening of the day on which Jesus rose from the dead two disciples were escaping Jerusalem and were making their way back to their home in a village called Emmaus. They were engaged in a heavy discussion on that road about what had been happening when a stranger caught them up and began to explain the events by referring them to the Scriptures. Later, after they had realized that the stranger had in fact been the risen Lord Jesus, they remembered how their hearts 'burned within them' as he unfolded the Scriptures for them.

When we engage in the Eucharist we are encountering mystery both in the sacrament and in the word and in each of these we meet with Jesus, living word and living bread. Before we go to the altar to receive the bread of life we gather round the Bible to share the word of life.

Hearing the Scriptures read and expounded takes us into all kinds of spiritual places: exultation, challenge and joy as well as questioning and doubt. Each of these is important in our Christian journey and in the deepening and maturing of our relationship with God. Taking the Bible seriously is essential for all Christians and finding ourselves familiar with it will only come when we have prayed our way through the word which reveals God.

In this chapter there are resources to help you engage with the Bible as we hear it read in church and as we read

it at home so that that word may be living and active
among us.

Entering into the mystery of God

Almighty God,
you have made us for yourself,
and our hearts are restless
till they find their rest in you:
pour your love into our hearts
and draw us to yourself,
and so bring us at last to your heavenly city
where we shall see you face to face;
through Jesus Christ our Lord. Amen.
       (*Common Worship*, after St Augustine)

Mysterious God,
you are beyond my imagining
yet I know you so well.
As I follow the mothers and fathers of faith
into the cloud of unknowing,
bring me to the place of revelation
where I shall see you face to face,
and with the saints and angels
worship you for all eternity. Amen.   (AN)

Lord, how much juice you can squeeze from a single
    grape!
How much water you can draw from a single well!
How great a fire you can kindle from a tiny spark!
How great a tree you can grow from a tiny seed!
My soul is so dry that by itself it cannot pray;
Yet you can squeeze from it
    the juice of a thousand prayers.
My soul is so parched that by itself it cannot love;
Yet you can draw from it boundless love for you
    and for my neighbour.

My soul is so cold that by itself it has no joy;
Yet you can light the fire of heavenly joy within me.
My soul is so feeble that by itself it has no faith;
Yet by your power my faith grows to a great height.
Thank you for prayer, for love, for joy, for faith;
Let me always be prayerful, loving, joyful, faithful.
(Guigo the Carthusian, died 1188)

O God, whose love is without measure: out of the depths
of my own creatureliness and yearning I call to you. Out
of your own immense depths of power and mystery
you call to me. Enable me to enter into the beginnings of
the secrets of your love, and let the poor stream of my
life flow into the immensity of your being.
(Brother Ramon SSF)

Almighty God,
give us wisdom to perceive you,
intellect to understand you,
diligence to seek you,
patience to wait for you,
eyes to behold you,
a heart to meditate upon you
and life to proclaim you,
through the power of the Spirit
of our Lord Jesus Christ.   (St Benedict, 480–c. 543)

Praying before you read the Bible

Blessed Lord,
who caused all holy Scriptures
to be written for our learning:
help us so to hear them,
to read, mark, learn and inwardly digest them
that, through patience,
and the comfort of your holy word,
we may embrace and for ever hold fast
the hope of everlasting life,

which you have given us in our Saviour Jesus Christ,
who is alive and reigns with you,
in the unity of the Holy Spirit,
one God, now and for ever. Amen.

(*Common Worship*)

O Lord,
open up your Word to us,
and our hearts to your Word;
that we may know you better
and love you more;
through Jesus Christ our Lord. Amen.

(James Ferguson)

Living Word,
you walked alongside your friends
and opened the Scriptures to them.
As I read your holy word,
accompany me
and open my heart and mind
that I may know you in your word
and find my life in you. Amen.   (AN)

Almighty God,
we invoke you,
the Fountain of everlasting light,
and ask you to send your truth into our hearts,
and to pour upon us the brightness of your glory,
through Jesus Christ our Lord. Amen.

(Use of Sarum)

Lord, as I read the psalms
let me hear you singing.
As I read your words,
let me hear you speaking.
As I reflect on each page,
let me see your image.

And as I seek to put your precepts into practice,
let my heart be filled with joy.
(St Gregory of Nazianzus, 329–389)

O Lord, you have given us your word
for a light to shine upon our path.
Grant us so to meditate on that word,
and to follow its teaching,
that we may find in it the light
that shines more and more until the perfect day;
through Jesus Christ our Lord.
Amen.
(*Common Worship*, after Jerome, *c.* 342–420)

Break through the thick darkness of our minds,
O Lord, with the bright rays of your Word,
that we may more fully know the truth
as it is in Jesus,
may mark with joy his footsteps,
and find in him the way to you.
For his Name's sake. Amen.   (James Ferguson)

Praying through the Bible

The Bible is a great source of prayer, and the following
are some of the prayers to be found in Scripture that can
inform our own prayer. Only one of the many possible
themes in each prayer is highlighted, but the full biblical
reference is given.

Christ's intercessory prayer

... that they may be one, as we are one.   (John 17)

The Lord's Prayer

Your will be done, on earth as it is in heaven.
(Matthew 6.9–15)

The tax collector's prayer of humility

God, be merciful to me, a sinner! (Luke 18.13)

Habakkuk's prayer of praise and awe

I stand in awe, O LORD, of your work.

(Habakkuk 3.2–19)

Ezra's prayer of contrition

O LORD, God of Israel, you are just. (Ezra 9.5–15)

Daniel's prayer for the people

O Lord, hear; O Lord, forgive; O Lord, listen and act and do not delay! (Daniel 9.4–19)

Hezekiah's prayer when sick

Remember now, O LORD, I implore you, how I have walked before you in faithfulness with a whole heart, and have done what is good in your sight. (Isaiah 38.3)

The prayer of Jabez for God's protection

Oh that you would bless me . . . and that your hand might be with me, and that you would keep me from hurt and harm! (1 Chronicles 4.10)

King Hezekiah's prayer of refuge to God

O LORD our God, save us, I pray you . . . so that all the kingdoms of the earth may know that you, O LORD, are God alone. (2 Kings 19.15–19)

Elijah's prayer at Mount Carmel

O LORD, God of Abraham, Isaac, and Israel, let it be known this day that you are God in Israel, that I am your servant, and that I have done all these things at your bidding.

(1 Kings 18.36–39)

Solomon's prayer of dedication

O hear in heaven your dwelling-place; heed and forgive.

(1 Kings 8.22–30)

David's prayer of thanks

You are great, O LORD God; for there is no one like you, and there is no God besides you.

(2 Samuel 7.18–29)

Abraham's prayer for Sodom

Shall not the Judge of all the earth do what is just?

(Genesis 18.23–25)

Stephen's prayer at his stoning

Lord Jesus, receive my spirit.   (Acts 7.59–60)

Paul's prayer for spiritual growth

I pray that you may have the power to comprehend, with all the saints, what is the breadth and length and height and depth, and to know the love of Christ that surpasses knowledge, so that you may be filled with all the fullness of God.   (Ephesians 3.14–21)

Paul's prayer for the knowledge of God's will

May you be made strong with all the strength that comes from his glorious power, and may you be prepared to endure everything with patience, while joyfully giving thanks to the Father, who has enabled you to share in the inheritance of the saints in the light.

(Colossians 1.9–12)

Paul's prayer for spiritual wisdom

I pray that the God of our Lord Jesus Christ, the Father of glory, may give you a spirit of wisdom and revelation as you come to know him, so that, with the eyes of your

heart enlightened, you may know what is the hope
to which he has called you, what are the riches of his
glorious inheritance among the saints, and what is the
immeasurable greatness of his power for us who believe,
according to the working of his great power.

(Ephesians 1.15–23)

Paul's prayer for partners in ministry

I long for all of you with the compassion of Christ Jesus.

(Philippians 1.3–11)

Being transformed by the Word

Merciful God,
teach us to be faithful in change and uncertainty,
that trusting in your word
and obeying your will
we may enter the unfailing joy
of Jesus Christ our Lord. Amen.

(*Common Worship: Additional Collects*)

May the words which I have read
take root in my heart
and change my life
for Jesus' sake. Amen.   (AN)

Almighty God, who hast taught us that not the hearers of
thy Word, but the doers, are justified in thy sight, grant
unto us that all our thoughts, words, and acts in private
and public, may be ever more in harmony with your
gracious will, through our Lord Jesus Christ. Amen.

(Rowland Williams, 1817–70)

Believing

Almighty and everlasting God,
you have given us your servants grace,
by the confession of a true faith,
to acknowledge the glory of the eternal Trinity
and in the power of the divine majesty to worship the
    Unity:
keep us steadfast in this faith,
that we may evermore be defended from all adversities;
through Jesus Christ your Son our Lord,
who is alive and reigns with you,
in the unity of the Holy Spirit,
one God, now and for ever.   (*Common Worship*)

Almighty God,
let not the flame of faith,
once kindled in our hearts,
be quenched for ever;
but do thou continually feed and renew it,
that it may ever shine
amid our darkness and groping,
until thou dost bring us to eternal life,
through Jesus Christ our Lord. Amen.
    (*Presbyterian Forms of Service*, 1899)

Almighty and eternal God,
you have revealed yourself
    as Father, Son and Holy Spirit,
and live and reign in the perfect unity of love:
hold us firm in this faith,
that we may know you in all your ways
and evermore rejoice in your eternal glory,

who are three Persons yet one God,
now and for ever. (*Common Worship*)

Let us not rest, O Lord, in a dead, ineffectual faith, but grant that it may be such as may show itself in good works, enabling us to overcome the world and to conform to the image of the Christ in whom we believe; for his Name's sake. Amen. (Dean Lancelot Addison, 1632–1703)

I believe; help my unbelief. (Mark 9.24)

Dear Lord, although I am sure of my position, I am unable to sustain it without you. Help me, or I am lost. Amen. (Martin Luther, 1483–1546)

Risen Jesus,
as you came to Thomas in his doubting
come to me now
and strengthen my weak faith. Amen. (AN)

O Christ, my Lord, again and again I have said with Mary Magdalene, 'They have taken away my Lord and I know not where they have laid him.' I have been desolate and alone. And thou hast found me again, and I know that what has died is not thou, my Lord, but only my idea of thee, the image which I have made to preserve what I have found, and to be my security. I shall make another image, O Lord, better than the last. That too must go, and all successive images, until I come to the blessed vision of thyself, O Christ, my Lord.

(George Appleton, 1901–93)*

My Lord God, I have no idea where I am going. I do not see the road ahead of me. I cannot know for certain where it will end. Nor do I really know myself, and the fact that I think I am following your will does not mean that I am actually doing so.

But I believe that the desire to please you does in fact please you. And I hope I have that desire in all that I am doing. I hope that I will never do anything apart from that desire. And I know that, if I do this, you will lead me by the right road, though I may know nothing about it.

Therefore I will trust you always though I may seem to be lost and in the shadow of death. I will not fear, for you are ever with me, and you will never leave me to face my perils alone. (Thomas Merton, 1915–68)

Hear us for those in our own land
who have never been taught the Faith;
for those who have rejected it,
or fallen away from it;
and for all who have no saving touch
    with thy Church,
and no trust in Christ.
Awaken all Christians so to present
the Lord Jesus Christ in word and deed,
that all the people may hear him gladly.
(James Ferguson)*

Prayer and the Holy Trinity

Christians believe in One God in Three Persons, the Father, Son and Holy Spirit. Prayer has a Trinitarian pattern: to the Father, through the Son and in the power of the Holy Spirit.

When we pray to the Father, we follow the example of Jesus. He prayed to his Father throughout his life and prays to him still.

We pray through the Son because Jesus has opened our way to God by his life, death and resurrection. We also talk about praying 'in the name' of Jesus. We use someone's name in this way to invoke his or her authority. An example is the paragraph in British passports requesting assistance for the traveller 'in the Name of Her Majesty'.

Jesus has ascended into heaven but he has not left us without a helper. He has sent the Holy Spirit to be our advocate and guide. In particular, the Holy Spirit gives us wisdom and courage to pray. St Paul wrote about this in the famous eighth chapter of his Letter to the Romans.

Prayer draws us into the life of God. God is life, through and through, because he is a relationship of love – the love of the Persons of the Holy Trinity.

5

Praying for the world

When we have heard the word of God our response is to pray together and that prayer is in the form of intercession. There are many kinds of prayer that we should properly offer and intercession is only one of them. Within our prayer life there should be praise and adoration, thanksgiving and penitence as well as praying for the specific needs of ourselves and others. Most often, though, we are drawn to holding before God in prayer the needs that we are so aware of. When we offer prayers on our own we may do so while lighting a candle; when we pray as a community we are invited to bring all our concerns together before the Lord as we are asked to pray 'for the Church and for the world and to thank God for his goodness'.

Prayer is part of the vocation of the Church and praying for one another is something that Christians have always done. In this chapter you will find prayers for specific needs as well as prayers for ourselves. In practice of course the intercessions also act as a reminder to us and a spur for action; our prayer leads into response so that we become, individually and as a community, part of God's response to the prayer that we in faith have offered.

As we pray we are also conscious that our prayer is caught up into the universal act of prayer that never ceases. As the popular hymn expresses it, 'the voice of prayer is never silent'. Earth resounds with prayer that echoes in heaven. We end our prayers by asking for the intercession of the saints who, in the words of St Thérèse of Lisieux, use their heaven in praying for us on earth.

This great and unceasing prayer of intercession is the spiritual equivalent of the friends who took apart the roof of the house where Jesus was staying to lower their friend to his feet (Mark 2.2–4). Their faith saved the sick man; our faith brings to the Lord all the things for which we would pray.

Beginning to pray

O Holy Spirit, giver of light and life,
impart to us thoughts better than our own thoughts,
and prayers better than our own prayers,
and powers better than our own powers,
that we may spend and be spent
in the ways of love and goodness,
after the perfect image of our Lord and Saviour
    Jesus Christ. Amen.
              (Eric Milner-White and G. W. Briggs)

O God, who hast ordained
that the prayers of thy Church
should open the way for thy blessing;
Help us to be intercessors with thee,
through Jesus Christ.   (James Ferguson)

Lord God, as I come into your presence,
still my body, open my heart and focus my mind,
that I may hear your Spirit drawing me closer to you.
Through Jesus the Lord. Amen.   (TW)

Almighty God,
who have called your people
to the ministry of intercession,

hear the prayers we offer up
in the Name of Christ.

(James Ferguson)*

O God, who spread your creating arms to the stars, strengthen our arms with power to intercede when we lift up
our hands unto you. (Armenian Liturgy)

All-purpose prayers

Be mindful, O Lord, of us your people,
present here before you,
and of those who are absent
through age, sickness, or infirmity.
Care for the infants,
guide the young,
support the aged,
encourage the faint-hearted,
collect the scattered,
and bring the wandering to your fold.
Travel with the voyagers,
defend the widows,
shield the orphans,
deliver the captives,
heal the sick.
Support all who are in danger, need or distress.
Remember for good all those who love us,
and those who hate us;
and those who have desired us,
unworthy as we are, to pray for them.
And those we have forgotten,
may you, O Lord, remember.
For you are the Helper of the helpless,
the Saviour of the lost,
the Refuge of the wanderer,
the Healer of the sick.
Just as you know each person's need,

and have heard their prayer,
grant to each according to your merciful
   loving-kindness
and your eternal love,
through Jesus Christ our Lord.
        (A Prayer of the Eastern Church)

The 'Universal prayer'

Lord, I believe in you: increase my faith.
I trust in you: strengthen my trust.
I love you: let me love you more and more.
I am sorry for my sins: deepen my sorrow.

I worship you as my first beginning,
I long for you as my last end,
I praise you as my constant helper,
And call on you as my loving protector.

Guide me by your wisdom,
Correct me with your justice,
Comfort me with your mercy,
Protect me with your power.

I offer you, Lord, my thoughts: to be fixed on you;
My words: to have you for their theme;
My actions: to reflect my love for you;
My sufferings: to be endured for your greater glory.

I want to do what you ask of me:
In the way you ask,
For as long as you ask,
Because you ask it.

Lord, enlighten my understanding,
Strengthen my will,
Purify my heart,
and make me holy.

Help me to repent of my past sins
And to resist temptation in the future.

Help me to rise above my human weaknesses
And to grow stronger as a Christian.

Let me love you, my Lord and my God,
And see myself as I really am:
A pilgrim in this world,
A Christian called to respect and love
All whose lives I touch,
Those under my authority,
My friends and my enemies.

Help me to conquer anger with gentleness,
Greed by generosity,
Apathy by fervour.
Help me to forget myself
And reach out toward others.

Make me prudent in planning,
Courageous in taking risks.
Make me patient in suffering,
unassuming in prosperity.

Keep me, Lord, attentive at prayer,
Temperate in food and drink,
Diligent in my work,
Firm in my good intentions.

Let my conscience be clear,
My conduct without fault,
My speech blameless,
My life well-ordered.
Put me on guard against my human weaknesses.
Let me cherish your love for me,
Keep your law,
And come at last to your salvation.

Teach me to realize that this world is passing,
That my true future is the happiness of heaven,
That life on earth is short,
And the life to come eternal.

Help me to prepare for death
With a proper fear of judgement,
But a greater trust in your goodness.
Lead me safely through death
To the endless joy of heaven.

Grant this through Christ our Lord. Amen.
(Attributed to Pope Clement XI, 1649–1721)

For the Church

Most gracious God,
we humbly pray for your holy catholic Church.
Fill it with all truth;
in all truth with all peace.
Where it is corrupt, purge it;
where it is in error, direct it;
where anything is amiss, reform it;
where it is right, strengthen and confirm it;
where it is in want, furnish it;
where it is divided, heal it,
and unite it in your love;
through Jesus Christ our Lord. Amen.
(Archbishop William Laud, 1573–1645)

Almighty and everlasting God, who formed your Church
to be of one heart and soul in the power of the resurrection and the fellowship of the Holy Spirit: renew her
evermore in her first love; and grant to your people such
a measure of your grace that their life may be hallowed,
their way directed, and their work made fruitful to the
good of your Church and the glory of your holy name;
through the same Jesus Christ our Lord.
(Community of the Resurrection)*

Remember in blessing thy whole Church,
and grant it purity of life and doctrine,
in purity peace,
in peace unity,

and in unity strength;
that thy saving power may be known over all,
and the whole world become
the happy Kingdom of thy Son.   (James Ferguson)

We pray you, Lord, to direct and guide your Church with
your unfailing care, that it may be vigilant in times of
quiet, and daring in times of trouble; through Jesus Christ
our Lord.   (*Franciscan Breviary*)

O God, who hast made thy Church on earth
as a bush that burns and is not consumed,
we beseech thee for all those whom thou
in the midst of this burning bush,
hast called to lead and serve thy people.
Cleanse the eyes of people everywhere
that they may see and discern thy Holy Fire
with which, in all ages, thy Church is aflame,
and that they may draw near with reverence,
because the place is holy ground.
                         (James Ferguson)*

For the unity of the Church

Lord Jesus Christ,
who said to your apostles,
'Peace I leave with you, my peace I give to you':
look not on our sins but on the faith of your Church
and grant it the peace and unity of your kingdom;
where you are alive and reign with the Father
in the unity of the Holy Spirit,
one God, now and for ever. Amen.
                         (*Common Worship*)

For the world

O God, the Father,
good beyond all that is good,
fair beyond all that is fair,

in whom is calmness, peace and concord,
mend the dissensions that divide us one from another,
and bring us back into a unity of love
which may bear some likeness to your divine nature.
Make us one in the fellowship of a good mind,
through that peace of yours
which makes all things peaceful,
and through the grace, mercy and tenderness,
by which you, O Lord,
are our Father for ever and ever.

(Jacobite Liturgy of St Dionysius)*

O Lord God,
who hast revealed to us
thy goodness and severity,
restrain with thy mercy
those who are tempted to evil.
Lift up the fallen,
redeem the enslaved,
and give searching of conscience
to those who deny thee.   (James Ferguson)

God our Creator,
who in making all things named them good,
we pray for your world,
that the goodness which is your gift
may overcome the seductions of greed and violence.
We pray for your world,
that the good which is our goal
may draw closer the dawn of your kingdom,
and restore us to your paradise. Amen.   (TW)

For the leaders of the world

Almighty God, the fountain of all goodness,
bless our Sovereign Lady, Queen Elizabeth,
and all who are in authority under her;
that they may order all things

in wisdom and equity, righteousness and peace,
to the honour and glory of your name,
and the good of your Church and people;
through Jesus Christ our Lord. Amen.

(*Common Worship*)

Lord God
we pray for those called
to positions of power and influence.
and especially for the leaders of the nations.
May they receive the
gift of holy wisdom,
and always be mindful of those in their care.
Through Jesus Christ our Lord. Amen.   (TW)

We pray for Elizabeth our Queen, for all lawful author-
ities, and for all the people of our land. Save us from the
evils that degrade our humanity and violate that which
is holy, and increase among us the zeal for justice,
true religion and kindness towards all.

(James Ferguson)*

For the environment

Creator God,
you made all things
and all you made was very good.
Show us how to respect
the fragile balance of life.
Guide by your wisdom those who have power
to care for or to destroy the environment,
that by the decisions they make
life may be cherished
and a good and fruitful earth
be preserved for future generations;
through Jesus Christ our Lord.
Amen.

(The Church of Scotland *Book of Common Order*)

God of justice,
Your Son Jesus Christ showed solidarity with the poor,
the weak and the vulnerable.
Give us the courage to do the same.
As homes are destroyed and lives
and livelihoods are lost,
help us to fight for a fair deal for the world's poor.
God of power,
time is running out.
Help us to reverse the tide of impending disaster,
and to play a part in your future.
God of hope,
in you we find abundant life.
May we work as a matter of urgency
to choose life over death
and to bring that life to your world.
God of love,
remind us that you are with us
as we seek to live differently;
challenge us to see how our actions
can change the world;
be with us as we act in your name.
Amen.   (Christian Aid)

For peace

Lord, make me an instrument of your peace;
where there is hatred, let me sow love;
where there is injury, pardon;
where there is doubt, faith;
where there is despair, hope;
where there is darkness, light;
and where there is sadness, joy.
Grant that I may not so much seek
to be consoled as to console;
to be understood, as to understand,
to be loved as to love;
for it is in giving that we receive,

it is in pardoning that we are pardoned,
and it is in dying that we are born to eternal life. Amen.
(Attributed to St Francis of Assisi, c. 1182–1226)

You can find more prayers for peace in Chapter 6.

For workers

Remember all working men and women
upon whose daily labour we depend,
and those who seek work and cannot find it.
Give us wisdom to create a world
in which there shall be no more want or oppression,
and where everyone shall eat the fruit of honest toil.
And give peace in the earth.   (James Ferguson)

For justice

Most merciful Father, you have called us to be a caring
Church, reflecting in our lives your infinite care for us
your children.

Help us to fulfil our calling and to care for one another
in an unselfish fellowship of love; and to care for the world
around us in sharing with it the good news of your love
and serving those who suffer from poverty, hunger and
disease.

We ask it in the name of Christ our Lord.
(Michael Ramsey, 1904–98)

God our deliverer,
defender of the poor and needy:
when the foundations of the earth are shaking
give strength to your people to uphold justice
and fight all wrong
in the name of your Son,
Jesus Christ our Lord.   (David Stancliffe)

O God the Father of all, you ask every one of us to
spread love where the poor are humiliated, joy where

the Church is brought low, and reconciliation where
people are divided, father against son, mother against
daughter, husband against wife, believers against those
who cannot believe, Christians against their unloved
fellow Christians. You open this way for us, so that the
wounded body of Jesus Christ, your Church, may be
leaven of communion for the poor of the earth and in
the whole human family.

(Blessed Teresa of Calcutta, 1910–97)

As I enter the street market
wheel my trolley at the superstore
leaf through a catalogue, or log on to the internet:
be with me and help me
when I spend money.
Be with me and help me
to see the marketplace as you see it,
as wide as the world you love so much.
Be with us and help us
to share the markets we share
for all people.
As we live under your steady gaze,
so we can change, by your gracious love.
Amen. (Christian Aid)

Creator God,
You loved the world into life.
Forgive us when our dreams of the future
are shaped by anything other
than glimpses of a kingdom
of justice, peace and an end to poverty.

Incarnate God,
you taught us to speak out for what is right.
Make us content with nothing less than a world
that is transformed into the shape of love,
where poverty shall be no more.

Breath of God,
let there be abundant life.
Inspire us with the vision of poverty over,
and give us the faith, courage and will
    to make it happen.   (Christian Aid)

For the forlorn

Compassionate God,
we pray for the forgotten peoples of your world,
for those unloved and all who live in despair.
By your power, transform your faithful people
to witness to your love for all creation. Amen.   (TW)

For those who care for others

We pray for all who seek to lift up the downtrodden,
and to befriend the outcast,
and for those who give up
earthly prospects and pleasant companionships,
in order to tend the weak,
to wait upon the sick,
and to comfort the lonely in their dying hours.
And we pray for all, who,
hurt and bruised in spirit,
serve without thanks,
and toil without recompense.
For them we know not what to ask,
but you know,
O Lover of souls.   (James Ferguson)*

For travellers

Almighty God, who alone can guard our coming in and
our going out, grant to all travellers, and those about to
travel, by land, sea or air, a prosperous journey, a quiet
time, a safe arrival at their journey's end, and a joyful
meeting with their friends to whom they go.
    (*The Priest's Prayer Book*)

For family, friends and neighbours

For the home

Almighty and everlasting God,
grant to this home the grace of your presence,
that you may be known to be
the inhabitant of this dwelling,
and the defender of this household;
through Jesus Christ our Lord,
who with you and the Holy Spirit
lives and reigns, one God,
for ever and ever.
Amen.

> (*The Book of Occasional Services*, 1994,
> of the Episcopal Church in the USA)

For family and friends

Into your strong hands, our Father,
we commend this day our souls and bodies,
our homes and families,
our friends and neighbours,
and all who specially need your help.
Grant to each of us your all-sufficient grace,
and keep us in peace and safety;
through Jesus Christ our Lord.
Amen.   (Douglas Horsefield)

For home and family

Merciful Saviour, who didst love Martha and Mary and
Lazarus, hallowing their home with thy sacred presence:
Bless, we beseech thee, our home, that thy love may rest
upon us, and that thy presence may be with us. May
we all grow in grace and in the knowledge of thee, our
Lord and Saviour. Teach us to love one another as thou
hast given commandment. Help us to bear one another's
burdens and so fulfil thy law, O blessed Jesus, who with

the Father and the Holy Spirit livest and reignest, one God,
for evermore. Amen.

(*Book of Common Prayer* of
the Anglican Church of Canada, 1959)

For family

Father in Heaven,
who by the grace of your Son Jesus Christ
has made us sons and daughters in the Family of God,
grant your blessing upon the families
to which by nature we belong;
cherish all our loved ones,
and bind us to one another
in those sacred bonds
that neither life nor death shall ever break.

(James Ferguson)*

For friends

May the God of all love,
who is the source of our affection
for each other formed here,
take our friendships into his keeping,
that they may continue and increase
throughout life and beyond it,
in Jesus Christ our Lord.
Amen.   (William Temple, 1881–1944)

Prayers for absent friends

God our Father,
you are present to your people everywhere.
We pray for those we love who are far away.
Watch over them and protect them.
Keep far from them
all that would hurt the body and harm the soul.
Give to them and to us
the assurance of your strength
and the peace of your presence,

and keep us all so near to you
that we will be for ever near to one another.
In your good time,
may we renew our fellowship on earth,
and at the last come to the unbroken fellowship
of the Father's house in heaven;
through Jesus Christ our Lord.
Amen.

(The Church of Scotland *Book of Common Order*)

O God, Who art everywhere present, look down with thy mercy upon those who are absent from among us. Give thy holy angels charge over them, and grant that they may be kept safe in body, soul and spirit, and presented faultless before the presence of thy glory with exceeding joy; through Jesus Christ our Lord. Amen.

(R. M. Benson, 1824–1915)

For those who are married

We thank you, most gracious God, for consecrating our marriage in Christ's Name and presence. Lead us further in companionship with each other and with you. Give us grace to live together in love and fidelity, with care for one another. Strengthen us all our days, and bring us to that holy table where, with those we love, we will feast for ever in our heavenly home; through Jesus Christ our Lord. Amen.

(*The Book of Occasional Services*, 1994,
of the Episcopal Church in the USA)

On a birthday

O Lord our heavenly Father, mercifully hear our prayers, and grant a long and happy life to thy servant *N.*, whose birthday we remember this day. May *he* grow in grace as *his* years increase, and ever live so as to please thee; in the power of thy Son, our Saviour Jesus Christ. Amen.

(*Book of Common Prayer*
of the Anglican Church of Canada, 1959)

For our enemies

Lord, who on the cross
prayed for your enemies,
give me the grace to pray for those who hate me,
for those who oppose me,
and those who make my life difficult.
As Herod and Pilate were reconciled
through your passion,
may I too be reconciled with my enemies
that I may live at peace with all. Amen.   (AN)

For those in need

God of all grace and comfort,
hear our prayer for those who are unhappy,
who are lonely or neglected,
who are damaged or abused,
or whose life is darkened
by fear or pain or sorrow.
Give us grace to help them when we can.
Give them faith
to look beyond their troubles to you,
their heavenly father and unfailing friend,
that they may take up the threads of life again
and go on their way with fresh courage
and renewed hope;
through Jesus Christ our Lord. Amen.
     (Church of Scotland *Book of Common Order*)

Prayer in time of economic crisis

God of plenty,
you have provided so much for us,
yet we have sought so much more for ourselves.
We have trusted in treasure on earth
when you have given us treasure in heaven.
We have built on sand
when we should have built on rock.
Open our eyes to recognize

what is of true and lasting value
and help us to invest
all we have and all we are
where true riches are to be found;
in Jesus' name. Amen. (AN)

Prayer for the unemployed

God of compassion,
your Son worked in the carpenter's shop
and moved among working men and women.
Strengthen those who have no work,
those who have lost their job,
those for whom the future of work seems uncertain.
Sustain their families,
restore their dignity,
and give them hope
in Jesus Christ our Lord. Amen. (AN)

Pray for the sick

Our Master, Jesus Christ,
visit the sick among your people and heal them. Amen.
(Abyssinian Jacobite Liturgy)

O Lord Jesus Christ,
Son of the living God,
set your passion, cross and death
between your judgement and our souls,
now and in the hour of our death.
Grant mercy and grace to the living,
rest to the departed,
to your Church peace and concord
and to us sinners forgiveness,
and everlasting life and glory;
for, with the Father and the Holy Spirit,
you are alive and reign,
God, now and for ever.
Amen.
(US Episcopal Church *Book of Common Prayer*, 1979)

Heavenly Father, who sent your Son
to be the Saviour of the body
as well as of the soul,
continue his gracious work,
we pray you,
among all who are oppressed by sickness.
Remember also those who are broken in their
    hearts,
or grieved in their minds;
the defeated and discouraged,
and all who have suffered loss or bereavement;
for whom we pray your fatherly comfort.

                        (James Ferguson)*

God of hope and healing
give courage to the sick,
patience to the suffering
and comfort to the anxious;
through Jesus Christ. Amen.   (AN)

Lord of our past, our present and our future
be with those whose memory has been taken
    from them,
who have lost a sense of who they are
and have forgotten who loves and cares for
    them.
As you brought order out of chaos,
calm anxious minds,
still their confusion
and bless them with your peace;
for though we may forget you
you will never forget us. Amen.   (AN)

Lord, I know that you care for me;
help me as I care for N. today.
When I am tired, give me strength;
when I am frustrated, give me patience;
when I am sad, give me hope;

and when the day is ending
give me the rest I need
to face tomorrow in your strength. Amen.   (AN)

A prayer for someone at the point of death, or immediately after

N., go forth upon your journey from this world,
in the name of God the Father almighty who created you;
in the name of Jesus Christ who suffered death for you;
in the name of the Holy Spirit who strengthens you;
in communion with the blessed saints,
and aided by angels and archangels,
and all the armies of the heavenly host.
May your portion this day be in peace,
and your dwelling the heavenly Jerusalem. Amen.

(Common Worship: Pastoral Services)

Pray for the dead

The Church has prayed for the dead since the earliest times. They were following a Jewish tradition, reflected in the holy books written just before the time of Jesus. We also see it in the Book of Job, where Job prays for his dead sons. There are many references to prayers for the dead in the writings of the Fathers.

C. S. Lewis made a good point when he said that prayer for the dead is the purest form of prayer. When we pray, we seek salvation for ourselves and others from God. The danger when we pray for the living is supposing that all we need is a little 'extra help' from God, although really we could get along fine without it. This is a mistake, and it is stripped away when we pray for the dead. Here, we ask God for something that clearly only he can do. Prayer for the dead is pure commendation. It is pure assent to a work that begins and ends with God.

It is traditional to pray for the departed in the days after a death and each year at the anniversary. They are also on our minds in November: the Commemoration of All Souls falls on the second day and lends its character to the whole month. The best prayer that we can offer for the dead is the Eucharist, where the living and the departed are joined together in Christ's death and Resurrection.

Almighty God,
we rejoice to know that your reign extends
far beyond the limits of this life.
In the mystery of what lies beyond our sight
we pray that your love may complete its work
in those whose days on earth are done;
and grant that we who serve you now in this world
may at last share with them
the glories of your heavenly kingdom;
through the love of Jesus Christ our Lord. Amen.
(Frank Colquhoun)

The Kontakion for the dead

Give rest, O Christ, to your servant with the saints:
where sorrow and pain are no more,
neither sighing, but life everlasting.

You only are immortal, the creator and maker of all:
and we are mortal, formed from the dust of the earth,
and unto earth shall we return.
For so you ordained when you created me, saying:
'Dust you are and to dust you shall return.'
All of us go down to the dust,
yet weeping at the grave we make our song:
Alleluia, alleluia, alleluia.

Give rest, O Christ, to your servant with the saints:
where sorrow and pain are no more,
neither sighing, but life everlasting.

(Eastern Orthodox prayer, translation
from *Common Worship: Pastoral Services*)

Heavenly Father,
into whose hands Jesus Christ
commended his spirit at the last hour:
into those same hands
we now commend your servant N,
that death may be for *him/her*
the gate to life and to eternal fellowship with you;
through Jesus Christ our Lord. Amen.

(*Common Worship: Pastoral Services*)

For anyone who has died

Lord, in your kindness have pity
on the soul of your servant N.
Grant to *him/her* eternal rest
through Christ, our Lord. Amen.   (AN)

Thanksgiving for the dead

Father of our spirits and God of love,
We give you thanks
for those most precious to our remembrance,
through whom you blessed our way:
our parents, brothers and sisters,
teachers and clergy
and friends,
who by faith have passed over the dark river
into the brightness of the Promised Land.

(James Ferguson)*

Praying for the departed at the end of your prayers

Rest eternal grant to them, O Lord,
and let light perpetual shine upon them.
May they rest in peace and rise in glory.
  (*Common Worship: Pastoral Services*)

Praying at a graveside

Risen Lord,
as your friends gathered at your tomb
the angel told them
'He is not here, he is risen.'
As I stand in this place of burial
I know that *N*. is not here
but awaiting the resurrection of all the faithful.
Yet while I wait
console me now
and give me peace. Amen.   (AN)

After you have been to a funeral

Almighty God, the Father of our Lord Jesus Christ,
whose disciples recognized him as he broke bread
    at their table after the resurrection:
we thank you for your strength upholding us
    in what we have done today,
and now we ask for your presence to be recognized
    in this home;
bring your peace and joy to each place which stirs the memory;
give your strength and presence in those daily tasks
    which used to be shared,
and in all the changes of life give us grace
    to do your will day by day,
and to look for the glorious coming of Christ,

when you will gather us together to your table in heaven
to be with you for ever and ever. Amen.

(Common Worship: Pastoral Services)

A prayer for faith

Heavenly Father,
in your Son Jesus Christ
you have given us a true faith and a sure hope.
Strengthen this faith and hope in us all our days,
that we may live as those who believe in
the communion of saints,
the forgiveness of sins
and the resurrection to eternal life;
through Jesus Christ our Lord. Amen.

(Common Worship: Pastoral Services)

Pray with the saints

Almighty and everlasting God,
who dost enkindle the flame of thy love
in the hearts of the Saints,
grant to our minds the same faith and power of love;
that as we rejoice in their triumphs,
we may profit by their examples;
through Jesus Christ our Lord. Amen.

(Gothic Missal)

*For additional prayers related to the saints and Our Lady
see Chapter 6.*

To end our prayers

Almighty God, the fountain of all wisdom, you know
our necessities before we ask, and our ignorance in
asking: have compassion on our weakness, and mercifully give us those things which for our unworthiness
we dare not, and for our blindness we cannot ask;

through the worthiness of your Son Jesus Christ our Lord.
Amen.

(Episcopal Church in the USA,
Book of Common Prayer, 1979)

Almighty God,
you have promised to hear the prayers
of those who ask in your Son's name;
we pray that what we have asked faithfully
we may obtain effectually;
through Jesus Christ our Lord. Amen.

(Common Worship)

Almighty God, who hast given us grace at this time with one
accord to make our common supplications unto thee; and
dost promise that when two or three are gathered together
in thy Name thou wilt grant their requests: fulfil now, O Lord,
the desires and petitions of thy servants, as may be most
expedient for them; granting us in this world knowledge of
thy truth, and in the world to come life everlasting. Amen.

(Prayer of St Chrysostom from
the Book of Common Prayer)

O God,
the Life of the faithful,
the Joy of your servants;
Receive the prayers of your people;
and may the souls which thirst for your promises,
be filled from your abundance;
through Jesus Christ our Lord. Amen.

(Gelasian Sacramentary)*

Upon the heavenly altar, high and lifted up, let the prayers
of your people constantly ascend, and hear the voice
of our thanksgivings and prayers, for your Name's sake,
O Lord, our Strength and our Redeemer.

(Liturgy of the Catholic Apostolic Church)*

Cease not thy pleading,
O Holy Spirit,
O Comforter eternal;
but when our love grows cold
and our prayer is dumb,
and we fall into the sleep of selfish care,
break in once more upon the darkness and void;
waken us to thy heavenly light
to know thee as the Life of our deepest life,
the Voice of our inmost conscience,
the Strength of our surrendered will.

(James Ferguson)*

Scriptural endings to prayer

To the King of the ages, immortal, invisible, the only God, be honour and glory for ever and ever. Amen.

(1 Timothy 1.17)

Now to him who by the power at work within us is able to accomplish abundantly far more than all we can ask or imagine, to him be glory in the church and in Christ Jesus to all generations, for ever and ever. Amen.

(Ephesians 3.20–21)

To him who is able to keep you from falling, and to make you stand without blemish in the presence of his glory with rejoicing, to the only God our Saviour, through Jesus Christ our Lord, be glory, majesty, power and authority, before all time and now and for ever. Amen.

(Jude 24–25)

The grace of the Lord Jesus Christ, the love of God, and the communion of the Holy Spirit be with all of you.

(2 Corinthians 13.13)

Orthodox ending for prayers

O Lord Jesus Christ, Son of God,
for the sake of the prayers of your most pure Mother,
    of Saint (*N., the name of the patron saint*),
of Saint (*N., the saint commemorated on this day*),
and of all your Saints,
have mercy upon us, and save us,
for you are a merciful God,
and you love all humankind. Amen.

                    (*A Manual of Eastern Orthodox Prayers*)*

6

Peace and reconciliation

———•◦•———

'Before you offer your gift at the altar, be reconciled with your brother and sister,' says Jesus (Matt. 5.24). In response to this command we share the peace. The act of doing so is part of the greater reconciliation that takes place in the Eucharist – the reconciliation between us and God, the reconciliation of us with our neighbours, the reconciliation of ourselves with ourselves. Disharmony occurs when there is a lack of peace and a community that is not at peace at any level cannot with all integrity go to the altar and share in the common bread and common cup. So we share the peace, with a handshake, with a kiss, or with a word, and it is genuine and heartfelt.

The Hebrew word *shalom* that we translate as peace is so much richer than our word would ever suggest. The Hebrew suggests wholeness, integrity, togetherness, a peace that passes all understanding. The sharing of such peace is a moment of profound joy, a moment of potential transformation.

The resources in this chapter will help us to think about this concept of peace in its broadest sense, including that wholeness of community that embraces the saints, the people of God of which we are part. At the peace we celebrate fellowship within the body of Christ. This fellowship includes the Church militant – those who are alive, the Church suffering – those who have died, and the Church triumphant – the saints in heaven. Being conscious of this fellowship encourages us in our living out of the peace we share.

Chief among the saints is the Blessed Virgin Mary, Our Lady, who is often styled 'Queen of Peace'. To her we have recourse as we ask her prayers for us and the whole Church at regular points in the day and in each of the seasons of the year. She, who is the mother of the One who guides our feet in the way of peace, sustains the Church through prayer.

Prayers for peace

O Almighty God,
the Father of all humanity,
turn, we pray, the hearts of all peoples and their rulers,
that by the power of your Holy Spirit
peace may be established among the nations
on the foundation of justice, righteousness and truth;
through him who was lifted up on the cross
to draw all people to himself,
your Son Jesus Christ our Lord. Amen.

(William Temple, 1881–1944)

Almighty God, from whom all thoughts of truth and peace proceed, kindle, we pray, in the hearts of all the true love of peace, and guide with your pure and peaceable wisdom those who take counsel for the nations of the earth; that in tranquillity your kingdom may go forward, until the earth is filled with the knowledge of your love; through Jesus Christ our Lord.

(Francis Paget, 1851–1911)

O God,
who would fold both heaven and earth
  in a single peace:
Let the design of thy great love

lighten upon the waste of our wraths and sorrows:
and give peace to thy Church,
peace among nations,
peace in our dwellings,
and peace in our hearts:
through thy Son our Saviour Jesus Christ. Amen.
(Eric Milner-White, 1884–1963)

O Christ, the peace of the things that are on high,
and the great rest of those that are below,
establish, O Lord, in thy peace and rest
the four regions of the world,
and principally thy holy Catholic Church.
Destroy wars and battles from the ends of the earth,
and disperse all those that delight in war;
and by thy divine mercy
pacify the Church and the Kingdom,
that we may have a safe habitation
in all soberness and piety.
And through thy merits and love
forgive the debts and sins
of them that are departed this life.
(Liturgy of Malabar)

O God,
the unsearchable abyss of peace,
the ineffable sea of love,
the fountain of blessings
and the bestower of affection,
giving peace to all who receive it;
Open to us this day the sea of your love
and water us with abundant streams
from the riches of your grace
and from the most sweet springs
    of your loving kindness.
Make us children of quietness and heirs of peace.
Kindle in us the fire of your love,

sow in us your fear,
strengthen our weakness by your power,
bind us closely to you and to each other
in our firm and indissoluble bond of unity.
                    (Syrian Clementine Liturgy)*

Christ our Hope,
we give you glory
for the great grace
by which upon the cross
you stretched out your hand in love to us all.
By that same grace
come, risen Saviour,
into every gesture of unity and fellowship
we make toward one another.
May the peace we share
be your peace. Amen.   (Jamie Wallace)

Praying with the communion of the saints

Our relation to the saints is summed up in one word
from the Nicene Creed: the word 'one'. There is only
one Church and it includes the living, the dead, and
those who are yet to be born. Christians have found
it natural to ask for the prayers of those who stand
before God in heaven, just as we ask for the prayers
of family and friends.

Some Christians since the Reformation have found
this difficult. They argue that the intercession of the
saints gets in the way of our relationship with God.
This can happen, but it does not need to. We ask
for the prayers of our living friends, and that does
not get in the way. Why should it when we ask for
the prayers of 'friends' who see God face to face? The

answer to every prayer comes from God, but in such a way as to involve us in one another's progress towards him. The journey through life is a communal one and praying for one another is a particularly important part of that.

We can ask for the prayers of anyone who has gone before us to God, but there is sense in asking for the prayers of those who lived particularly holy lives. The Letter of St James tells us that 'the prayer of a righteous person has great effect' (James 5.16). Among the vast company of the saints, certain ones stand out. We ask for the prayers of the Virgin Mary most of all because of her closeness to Jesus as his mother. We might also invoke the saint whose name we share, if there is such a saint, or of the saint whose feast we celebrate on a particular day. We might add the patron of our parish church, or a saint associated with the concern we have in mind: the 'patron saint'.

St Paul tells us to mourn with those who mourn and rejoice with those who rejoice. Prayer and thanksgiving are one important way in which we do that. We do it in the company of Mary and John, and Peter and Paul, and the whole company of heaven.

Byzantine Orthodox Prayer to the Saint whose Name you bear

Pray to God for me, O Saint N.,
well-pleasing to God,
I come to you eagerly,
the speedy helper and intercessor for my soul.
        (*A Manual of Eastern Orthodox Prayers*)*

The earliest known prayer to Our Lady, *Sub tuum praesidium* (*c.* 250)

Beneath your compassion,
We take refuge, O Mother of God.
Despise not our prayers in time of trouble
But rescue us from dangers,
Who alone are pure, alone are blessed.

An Orthodox prayer to the Mother of God

Into his joy, the Lord has received you,
Virgin God-bearer, Mother of Christ.
You have beheld the King in his beauty,
Mary, daughter of Israel.
You have made answer for the creation
To the redeeming will of God.
Light, fire and life, divine and immortal,
Joined to our nature you have brought forth,
That to the glory of God the Father,
Heaven and earth might be restored.
(By the Benedictine Community
at St Mary's Abbey, West Malling)

Anthems to Our Lady through the year, traditionally said in the late evening

Alma Redemptoris Mater (Advent to Candlemas)

Mother of Christ, hear thou thy people's cry,
Star of the deep and portal of the sky!
Mother of Him, who thee from nothing made,
Sinking we strive and call to thee for aid:
Oh, by that joy which Gabriel brought to thee,
Thou Virgin first and last, let us thy mercy see.
(Translated by Edward Caswall, 1814–78)

Ave, Regina caelorum (Candlemas to Holy Week)

Hail, Queen of Heaven, beyond compare
to whom the angels homage pay;
hail, Root of Jesse, Gate of light,
that opened for the world's new day.
Rejoice, O Virgin unsurpassed,
in whom our ransom was begun,
for all your loving children pray
to Christ, our Saviour, and your Son.
                (Translation from Stanbrook Abbey)

Regina caeli (Eastertide)

Joy to thee, O Queen of Heaven. Alleluia!
He whom thou wast meet to bear. Alleluia!
As he promised hath arisen. Alleluia!
Pour for us to God thy prayer. Alleluia!
                        (Traditional translation)

Salve Regina (Ordinary time)

Hail our Queen and Mother blest!
Joy when all was sadness,
Life and hope you give mankind,
Mother of our gladness!
Children of the sinful Eve,
Sinless Eve, befriend us,
Exiled in this vale of tears,
Strength and comfort send us!
Pray for us, O Patroness,
Be our consolation!
Lead us home to see your Son,
Jesus, our salvation!
Gracious are you, full of grace,
Loving as none other,
Joy of heaven and joy of earth,
Mary, God's own Mother!   (*The Divine Office*)

The Angelus

The tradition among many Christians is to remember three times each day the wonder of the Incarnation. Traditionally this has been done by saying the Angelus at 6 a.m., at noon and at 6 p.m. The words of the Angelus are drawn from Scripture. The church bell is rung in a rhythmic pattern – three times for each part of the Angelus and three times while the final prayer is being said. At home or work the times might not suit our pattern of living or there will be no bells to summon us to pray – but we can set our own time and our own way of reminding ourselves.

V. The Angel of the Lord brought tidings to Mary.
R. And she conceived by the Holy Spirit.
Hail Mary, full of grace, the Lord is with you. (Luke 1.28)
Blessed are you among women, and blessed is the fruit of your womb, Jesus. (Luke 1.42)
Holy Mary, Mother of God, pray for us sinners, now and at the hour of our death. Amen.

V. Behold the handmaid of the Lord.
R. Be it unto me according to your Word.
Hail Mary . . .

V. And the Word was made flesh.
R. And dwelt among us.
Hail Mary . . .

V. Pray for us, O Holy Mother of God.
R. That we may be made worthy of the promises of Christ.

Let us pray:
We beseech you, O Lord,
pour your grace into our hearts,
that as we have known the incarnation
    of your Son Jesus Christ
by the message of an angel,
so by his cross and passion

we may be brought to the glory of his resurrection;
through Jesus Christ our Lord. Amen.

In Eastertide the Angelus is replaced by the *Regina caeli*.
This is often sung to the tunes of the hymns 'Jesus Christ
is risen today' after Easter and then 'Hail the day that sees
him rise' after the Ascension and through to Pentecost.

Joy to you, O Queen of Heaven, alleluia:
He whom you were fit to bear, alleluia,
As he promised has arisen, alleluia.
Pour for us to God your prayer, alleluia.

V. Rejoice and be glad, O Virgin Mary, alleluia.
R. For the Lord has risen indeed, alleluia.

Let us pray:
O God, you gave joy to the world through the resurrection
of your Son our Lord Jesus Christ; grant, we pray you, that
through the intercession of the Virgin Mary, his Mother,
we may obtain the joys of everlasting life, through the
same Christ our Lord. Amen.

7

Prayers at meals

———•◆•———

The miracle of God is that he takes what we give and does amazing things with it. God takes the bread and the wine that we place on the altar and he gives us the body and blood of his dear Son. God takes the offerings of our lives and transforms them by his grace. Our money, our time, our talents, all that we are is offered at the altar as a 'living sacrifice'. Out of such meagre gifts God builds his Church.

What we give in church should be the result of as careful consideration as what we give to the person we most love at Christmas or their birthday. We think long and hard about what they would like, what they would enjoy and what we can afford and we are thrilled and excited when we find the right thing. Our giving to the Church, to God, should never be the result of casual thinking but of prayerful planning and deliberate response. We give in response to what we have received, generous love responding to generous love. This is planned giving, this is real stewardship and this should be as much part of the way in which we live as Christians as how often we read the Bible or come to Mass.

In this chapter there are resources to help you pray about what you give and what you offer and there are also prayers of thanksgiving in response to what you have received. Part of that thanksgiving happens whenever we gather at a table. No meal should pass without thanksgiving and without a remembrance that 'all things come from you and of your own do we give you'.

Our offering will always feel inadequate in response to what God has given to us, but Jesus took the offering of loaves and fishes from a small boy and fed a multitude with them. He will take what you give and do mighty things with them.

Offertory prayers

Be present, be present,
Lord Jesus Christ,
our risen high priest;
make yourself known
in the breaking of bread. Amen.   (*Common Worship*)

Stewardship prayers

Lord Jesus Christ,
by taking human flesh you sanctified material things
to be a means of your grace;
grant us wisdom in our attitude to money,
and a generous heart in the use
of the resources entrusted to us,
that by faithful stewardship we may glorify you.
   Amen.

(Adapted from a prayer from
the C. of E. Central Board of Finance)

Generous God, you are Life:
Life that gives itself,
Returns upon itself
And pours itself out afresh:
God the Holy Trinity.
You have made us
In your image.

Help us to live with
Generosity and commitment
As our priority too.
May our praise and thanksgiving
Be shown not only with our lips,
But in our lives:
Through our time, our purses,
Our skills and our prayer. Amen.
(General Synod of the Scottish Episcopal Church)

Generous God,
you have given everything to me;
accept the offering I make to you today,
and with my gift
accept the offering of my life. Amen.   (AN)

Prayers at meals

Be present at our table, Lord
Be here and everywhere adored
Thy mercies bless and grant that we
May strengthened for thy service be. Amen.
(Robert Burns, 1759–96)

Good Lord, bless these sinners
as they eat their dinners. Amen.   (Traditional)

For Bacon, Eggs and Buttered Toast,
Praise Father, Son and Holy Ghost. Amen.
(Traditional)

For food in a world where many walk in hunger;
For faith in a world where many walk in fear;
For friends in a world where many walk alone;
We give you humble thanks, O Lord. Amen.
(Huron Hunger Fund,
Anglican Church of Canada)

Prayer before a meal

The eyes of all wait upon you, O God,
And you give them their food in due season.
You open wide your hand
and fill all things living with plenteousness.

Bless, O Lord, these gifts to our use
and us in your service;
relieve the needs of those in want
and give us thankful hearts;
for Christ's sake. Amen.

Prayer after a meal

All your works praise you, O God,
And your faithful servants bless you.
They make known the glory of your kingdom
And speak of your power.

For these and all God's gifts and graces,
let us bless the Lord.
Thanks be to God.
(*Celebrating Common Prayer: The Pocket Version*)

Bless the Lord, O my soul,
And all that is within me,
bless his holy name.
Bless the Lord, O my soul,
And forget not all his benefits.

Blessed be God, eternal king,
for these and all his good gifts to us. Amen.
(*Celebrating Common Prayer: The Pocket Version*)

Without ceasing

St Paul tells us that we should 'pray without ceasing'. This sounds like an impossible feat, but there are several ways we can enter into the spirit of constant prayer.

Although we cannot pray absolutely all the time, we can pray often. Throughout the day we can offer whatever it is that we are doing to God, and thank him for all the good that comes our way. We can pray at the beginning of the day and at the end, before setting out on a journey and on arriving, before meals and before work or study.

As important as praying often is praying in a regular and committed way. If we go to Mass every Sunday, and say prayers of some form at the beginning and end of every day, then our life takes on a prayed-in character. It has this quality when we are praying and in the time in between, when we are not.

In prayer we turn our thoughts to God, asking him to forgive our sins and aid us in our weakness. We can pray without ceasing by asking God to see our constant need as a constant prayer: 'Lord, may the poverty of my soul stand before you as my intercession.'

Finally, let us not forget that prayer is the communal work of the whole Church. We each play our part in corporate prayer and worship. This prayer is quite literally always being made to God from his Church around the world. As the hymn has it: 'The voice of prayer is never silent, | Nor dies the strain of praise away.'

8

Thanksgiving and the Holy Spirit

———◆◦◆———

The Greek word *eucharistia* means thanksgiving and so the Eucharist is wholly an act of thanksgiving. But at the heart of the liturgy is what is often called the Prayer of Thanksgiving or the Eucharistic Prayer. This prayer is prayed by the president on behalf of the whole people of God gathered around the altar. It's a prayer in which we all take part, acting like a chorus, responding in dialogue with the priest, interspersing heaven's songs with our earthly worship, remembering the great mystery of our faith and joining in a resounding 'Amen', let it be so.

The structure of the Prayer of Thanksgiving is both ancient and important. We have a great variety of prayers in the Church of England rites but each contains the same elements. We begin by remembering what God has done for us, principally in Jesus Christ, and we remember that when we worship we are echoing worship that is going on in heaven 'with angels and archangels and all the company' gathered there. We then ask that God will send his Spirit on the gifts that are on the altar, the bread and the wine. Then we remember what happened at the last supper, using the Lord's own words, an act of remembrance that makes the events then real now. Finally, the prayer concludes with a great act of *anamnesis*, remembrance, when we recall the nature of what we do, of what God has done and the effect that all this will have.

In this chapter you will find prayers that reflect something of these elements and which can help us to be thankful people, both at the Eucharist and in our everyday lives. But perhaps most importantly, this is not the time in the Mass to be wrapped up in our own devotions but to be absorbed in adoration of the God who is present with us. Our hearts should beat with the beat of the Mass as our eyes are drawn from the earthly to the heavenly altar and as with Thomas we can make the simplest yet most profound declaration of faith as we too see Jesus – 'My Lord and my God'.

Prayers of thanksgiving

Lord Jesus Christ, we thank you
for all the benefits you have won for us,
for all the pains and insults you have borne for us.
Most merciful redeemer,
friend and brother,
may we know you more clearly,
love you more dearly,
and follow you more nearly,
day by day. Amen.
(St Richard of Chichester, 1197–1253)

We thank thee, O Lord our Lord,
for our being, our life, our gift of reason;
for our nurture, our preservation and guidance;
for our education, civil rights and religious privileges;
for thy gifts of grace, of nature, of this world;
for our redemption, regeneration,
and instruction in the Christian Faith;
for our calling, recalling,
and our manifold renewed recalling,
for thy forbearance and long-suffering,
thy prolonged forbearance

many a time and many a year.
For all the benefits we have received,
and all the undertakings wherein we have prospered;
for any good we may have done;
for the use of the blessing of this life;
for thy promise,
and our hope of the enjoyment
    of good things to come;
for good and honest parents,
gentle teachers, benefactors ever to be remembered,
congenial companions, intelligent hearers,
sincere friends, faithful servants;
for all who have profited us by their writings,
sermons, conversations, prayers,
examples, reproofs, injuries.
For all these, and also for all other mercies,
known and unknown, open and secret,
remembered by us or now forgotten,
kindnesses received by us willingly
or even against our will:
We praise thee, we bless thee, we thank thee,
and will praise and bless and thank thee
all the days of our life;
through Jesus Christ our Lord. Amen.
                    (Bishop Lancelot Andrewes, 1555–1626)

We thank you for the glory of the world
which you have made,
for dawn and sunset,
the light of the moon,
the gleaming constellations,
the ebb and flow of the sea,
for the sense of mystery
that fills the vast immensity of space,
and the unfathomable depth of the soul.

For all knowledge and art
which finds its inspiration in you:

for books, music, form, and colour,
for crafts and the works of human hands.

Yet more we praise you
for love and homes,
for the glance of kindly eyes,
and the constancy of brave hearts,
that shine in the darkness like the stars of heaven,
and point the way that leads home to you.

And above all, we thank you
for the unfolding of your love in Jesus Christ,
who came to bear the burden of our life,
and to die for our salvation.

Thanks be to God for his unspeakable gift,
through Jesus Christ our Lord. Amen.

(James Ferguson)*

The General Thanksgiving

Almighty God, Father of all mercies, we thine unworthy servants do give thee most humble and hearty thanks for all thy goodness and loving-kindness to us, and to all men; We bless thee for our creation, preservation, and all the blessings of this life; but above all for thine inestimable love in the redemption of the world by our Lord Jesus Christ, for the means of grace, and for the hope of glory. And we beseech thee, give us that due sense of all thy mercies, that our hearts may be unfeignedly thankful, and that we shew forth thy praise, not only with our lips, but in our lives; by giving up ourselves to thy service, and by walking before thee in holiness and righteousness all our days; through Jesus Christ our Lord, to whom with thee and the Holy Ghost be all honour and glory, world without end. Amen.

(Book of Common Prayer, 1662)

Praying with angels and archangels

Holy, holy, holy God
surrounded by angels
praised by saints
adored by all
may I know that
the angels protect me
the saints pray for me
and heaven lies before me
this day and for ever. Amen.　　(AN)

Holy Guardian Angel,
be beside me today/tonight
watch my steps
and keep me safe
and if I should forget you
don't forget me. Amen.　　(AN)

O Master, our Lord and our God,
who established in the heavens
orders and hosts of Angels and Archangels
for the service of your glory:
grant that your holy angels may enter with us
　　here,
serving with us, and glorifying with us your
　　goodness.
　　　　　　　(Liturgy of St John Chrysostom)*

Prayer to Michael and the other Archangels

Supreme Leaders of the Heavenly Hosts,
we implore you,
encircle us with your prayers,
unworthy as we are,
and protect us under the wings
of your immaterial glory.
Guard us who fall down before you
and fervently cry:

deliver us from dangers,
commanders of the powers above.
(*A Manual of Eastern Orthodox Prayers*)*

Prayers for the descent of the Holy Spirit

O Holy Spirit, the Comforter,
with the Father and the Son ever one God,
descend into our hearts
that while you make intercession for us,
we may today with confidence call upon our Father;
through Jesus Christ our Lord. Amen.
(Mozarabic Liturgy)*

Heavenly King,
Comforter and the Spirit of Truth;
Present everywhere and filling all things,
Treasury of blessings and Giver of Life:
Come and dwell in us,
Cleanse us from every sin,
And save our souls
For you are good to all.
(Eastern Orthodox Prayer)

O thou who camest from above,
the pure celestial fire to impart,
kindle a flame of sacred love
on the mean altar of my heart.

There let it for thy glory burn
with inextinguishable blaze,
and trembling to its source return
in humble prayer, and fervent praise.
(Charles Wesley, 1707–88)

Come, Holy Spirit, fill the hearts
of your faithful people,
and kindle in them the fire of your love.   (Traditional)

Veni, Creator Spiritus

Come, Holy Ghost, our souls inspire,
and lighten with celestial fire.
Thou the anointing Spirit art,
who dost thy sevenfold gifts impart.

Thy blessèd unction from above
is comfort, life, and fire of love.
Enable with perpetual light
the dullness of our blinded sight.

Anoint and cheer our soilèd face
with the abundance of thy grace.
Keep far our foes, give peace at home:
where thou art guide no ill can come.

Teach us to know the Father, Son,
and thee, of both, to be but One,
that through the ages all along,
this may be our endless song:

Praise to thy eternal merit,
Father, Son, and Holy Spirit. Amen.
(attributed to Rabanus Maurus,
c. 780–856, trans. John Cosin, 1594–1672)

An invocation to the Holy Spirit

Come, true light.
Come, eternal life.
Come, hidden mystery.
Come, treasure without name.
Come, reality beyond all words.
Come, person beyond all conceiving.
Come, rejoicing without end.
Come, light that knows no evening.
Come, unfailing expectation of the saved.
Come, raising of the fallen.
Come, resurrection of the dead.
Come, all-powerful, for unceasingly
you create, refashion and change all things
by your will alone.
Come, invisible whom none may touch and handle.
Come, for you continue always unmoved,
yet at every instant you are wholly in movement;
you draw near to us who lie in hell,
yet you remain higher than the heavens.
Come, for your name fills our hearts with longing,
and is ever on our lips;
yet who you are and what your nature is,
we cannot say or know.
Come, alone to the alone.
Come, for you are yourself
the desire that is within me.
Come, my breath and my life.
Come, the consolation of my humble soul.
Come, my joy, my glory, my endless delight.
                    (St Symeon the New Theologian,
                    949–1022, trans. Kallistos Ware)

Prayer and the offering of the Mass

The Mass – which is another name for the Eucharist – is the greatest prayer of the Church. Prayer brings us in touch with God; at the Eucharist, God gives himself to us in the Body and Blood of Christ. Whenever we pray, we can come before God because Christ offered himself for us on the cross. In the Eucharist, Christ's sacrifice is made present upon the altar. As the hymn writer William Bright put it, it is the moment when we have with us 'Him that pleads above'.

The Mass is the best place of all to bring our prayers before God, for ourselves, the world and those we love. There is a good tradition of going to Mass with a particular concern or 'intention' on our minds. It is good to remember this before God during the consecration or at the Agnus Dei. We can also ask the priest to remember someone or something at the altar. We call this 'offering a Mass' – for someone who has died, for instance, or for someone who is sick. And the Mass is not only for sad things. Traditionally, when Christians have something to be thankful for, they give money to charity and they ask for a Mass to be said. It is the perfect way to give thanks for the birth of a child, or a wedding anniversary.

9

Praying the Our Father

The most important part of the Lord's Prayer is the opening words 'Our Father'. This is the corporate prayer which Jesus himself gives to the Church and which the Church prays between the great act of Thanksgiving and the receiving of communion. Each time we pray 'Our Father' we remember our personal relationship with God. We share in the relationship with our Father as brothers and sisters and we share in the sacrament, one bread, as one body. In order to share the bread it must be broken, but that act of breaking the bread also reinforces our sense of being one body.

The prayers in this chapter remind us that it is not only bread that is broken and that we need that broken bread for the journey that lies before us if we are to live with our own brokenness. There are many whose lives are broken, shattered through what they have experienced. There are many communities that are broken, many places where fragmentation has taken place. Christ, broken on the cross, Christ, the bread of life broken on the altar, speaks to us in our broken state. It was when the Lord took bread at the table at Emmaus and broke it that the eyes of the two disciples were opened and they recognized the presence of the Lord. It is often in situations of brokenness that we recognize Jesus in the midst.

We serve the Lord where we find him among his broken people, in the sick, in the homeless, in those in prison, the naked, the abandoned – Jesus is one with them, to whom we minister as we minister to the broken. The faith we share and which we express together in the Mass brings us into solidarity with all people in their joy and in their pain, and we find all our lives offered and redeemed on the altar.

Praying the Lord's Prayer

A prayer inspired by the Lord's Prayer

God, lover of us all,
most holy one,
help us to respond to you,
to create what you want for us here on earth.
Give us today enough for our needs;
forgive our weak and deliberate offences,
just as we must forgive others when they hurt us.
Help us to resist evil and to do what is good;
for we are yours,
endowed with your power
to make our world whole.   (Lala Winkley)

An Orthodox introduction to the Lord's Prayer

O God, the Father of our Lord Jesus Christ,
blessed by cherubim and seraphim,
exalted by thousands and myriads
of heavenly and rational hosts,
sanctifier and perfecter
of the offerings and fruits offered to you;
sanctify our bodies, minds, souls and spirits
that we may with pure hearts and unashamed faces
call upon you,
O God and heavenly Father, saying: *Our Father . . .*
(Liturgy of St James, Antiochian Catholic
Church in America)

Breaking the bread

We give thanks to you, our Father,
For the holy vine of David your servant
which you have revealed to us
through Jesus your servant.
To you be glory for ever.
We give thanks to you, our Father,
For the life and knowledge,
which you have revealed to us
through Jesus your servant.
To you be glory for ever.
As this fragment
lay scattered upon the mountains
and has been gathered to become one,
so gather your Church
from the ends of the earth
into your kingdom.
For the glory and power are yours,
through Jesus Christ, forever. Amen.   (From the *Didache*)

For the fragments

Jesus, on the hillside you said
'Gather the fragments
that nothing may be lost'.
May I never forget the fragments
broken people
broken communities
broken lives
broken environment.
May nothing created
ever be lost. Amen.   (AN)

A prayer for broken people

Lord Jesus, as the bread is broken in the Eucharist
you were broken on the cross.
Have compassion on the broken people of our
    world

those who have been damaged by life
by things said to them
by things done to them.
In your love
heal them and make them whole. Amen.   (AN)

Food for the journey

God of our pilgrimage
as you fed your people with manna for their journey
so feed us that we may walk
the way of our earthly pilgrimage
and come at last to our promised land with you
where you reign for ever. Amen.   (AN)

Let us make our way together, Lord; wherever you go
I must go: and through whatever you pass, there too I
will pass.   (Teresa of Avila, 1515–82)

My spirit has become dry because it forgets to feed on you.
                         (St John of the Cross, 1542–91)

With bread from heaven and water from the
    rock
you satisfied the hunger and thirst of your
    children.
Lord, satisfy my hunger,
quench my thirst,
as I come to you in this Eucharist. Amen.   (AN)

Preparation for death

Grant, O Lord,
that we may live in your fear,
die in your favour,
rest in your peace,
rise in your power,

reign in your glory;
for the sake of your Son,
Jesus Christ our Lord. Amen.
(Archbishop William Laud, 1573–1645)*

From thee we came.
Into thy hands we must fall at last.
Let it not be with misused powers
and sad decay,
but in the fullness
of ripened faith and hope.   (John Hunter)

O God,
who has given us both the power
and the opportunity to do well,
grant that before our day is done,
we may have performed some good work,
whose fruit shall remain,
and then of your great mercy
let us depart in peace,
because our eyes have seen your salvation. Amen.
(James Ferguson)

O, my Lord and Saviour, support me in that hour in the
strong arms of thy sacraments, and by the fresh fragrance
of thy consolation. Let the absolving words be said
over me, and the holy oil sign and seal me, and thy
own Body be my food, and thy Blood my sprinkling;
and let my sweet Mother, Mary, breathe on me, and
my Angel whisper peace to me, and my glorious Saints
smile upon me: that in them all, and through them all, I
may receive the gift of perseverance, and die, as I desire
to live, in thy faith, in thy Church, in thy service, and in
thy love.

(John Henry Newman, 1801–90)

Eternal God, on you have I depended from my mother's womb, you have I loved with all the strength of my soul, to you have I dedicated my flesh and my soul from my youth until now. Set by my side an angel of light, to guide me to the place of repose, where are the waters of rest, among the holy Fathers. You have broken the fiery sword and restored to Paradise the thief who was crucified with you and implored your mercy: remember me also in your kingdom, for I too have been crucified with you. Let not the dread abyss separate me from your elect. Let not the envious one bar the way before me. But forgive me and accept my soul into your hands, spotless and undefiled, as incense in your sight.

(St Macrina, *c.* 327–79, as given in her *Life*,
by St Gregory of Nyssa)

Prayer with others

The definitive Christian prayer is with other people. We meet together and Jesus is with us – even, he says, when only two or three are gathered in his name. The supreme form of prayer together is the liturgy of the Church: this is our Common Worship and Common Prayer. This praying together does not need to be in a church building. It can happen wherever we are – maybe, for instance, at a weekly prayer meeting where we work.

Even when we are 'by ourselves' our prayer is prayer with others. We pray as part of a company too large to count, of angels and saints. We pray with Christians of every age and with our brothers and sisters throughout the world. The anchor of this community of prayer are the members of religious orders – the men and women who have vowed themselves to a life of prayer and contemplation. When we feel alone in prayer, we can remember them. For some people this link is particularly important, and they join a religious community as a 'tertiary' or 'oblate'. They belong to the order as a layperson or member of the parish clergy and follow a version of the community's rule of life.

10

Communion and the Sacrament

———•·•·•———

Receiving communion, receiving the sacrament of the Lord's body and blood is the climax of the Eucharist. Breaking the word and breaking the bread have brought us to the altar. With empty hands we reach out to receive what God freely gives to us, unworthy as we are, though reconciled to him and at peace with one another and ourselves. The act of communion is of course corporate. The bread was broken so that one loaf can feed us all. Yet there is something of personal encounter at this supreme moment within the service.

However often we make our communion it is hard to understand what it is that we are doing, what a profound and life-changing moment this is. This 'outward and visible sign of inward and spiritual grace' is God present with us, God feeding us with his own self to sustain us in our daily living. This is the 'daily bread' for which we have prayed to our Father.

No sacrament should be received casually, without preparation, without serious thought. Preparing to make our communion should be part of what we do before we come to church and while we are worshipping but also as we approach the altar and as the host is placed in our hands and the cup touches our lips. In this chapter there are prayers to help us with this essential preparation.

There may be times when we cannot get to Mass and we may be using the prayers in this book to help us participate in a service that is taking place elsewhere. In such an instance we then make a spiritual communion, knowing that God will fill us with the grace which is his free gift in this sacrament.

Wherever we are this moment takes us to that upper room and to the table with the disciples knowing that as often as we eat and drink we proclaim the Lord's death until he comes.

Prayer as you receive communion

My Lord and my God! (John 20.28)

O God,
who hast called us to open our hand,
and thou wouldest fill it,
and we would not;
open thou not only our hand,
but our heart also;
that we may know nothing but thee,
count all things lost in comparison of thee,
and endeavour to be made like unto thee;
through Jesus Christ our Lord.
(Jeremy Taylor, 1613–67)

Almighty God,
who fillest all things with thy boundless Presence,
yet makest thy chosen dwelling-place in the human soul;
Come thou, a gracious and willing Guest,
take thine abode in our hearts;
and at thy coming let all unholy thoughts and desires
that lodge within us
be cast out and depart;
and thy Holy Presence be to us
comfort, light and love;
through Jesus Christ our Lord. Amen.
(James Ferguson)

Prayers of adoration

O sacred banquet,
in which Christ is received,
the memory of his Passion is recalled,
the mind is filled with grace,
and a token of future glory is given to us.
                    (St Thomas Aquinas, 1225–74)

Lord Jesus Christ,
we thank you that in this wonderful sacrament
you have given us the memorial of your passion:
grant us so to reverence the sacred mysteries
of your body and blood
that we may know within ourselves
and show forth in our lives
the fruit of your redemption;
for you are alive and reign,
now and for ever. Amen.   (*Common Worship*)

The divine praises, traditionally prayed before the Blessed Sacrament

Blessed be God.
Blessed be his Holy Name.
Blessed be Jesus Christ, true God and true man.
Blessed be the name of Jesus.
Blessed be his most Sacred Heart.
Blessed be Jesus in the most holy Sacrament
     of the Altar.
Blessed be the Holy Spirit, the Paraclete.
Blessed be the great Mother of God,
     Mary most holy.
Blessed be her holy and Immaculate Conception.
Blessed be her glorious Assumption.
Blessed be the name of Mary, Virgin and
     Mother.

Blessed be Saint Joseph, her most chaste spouse.
Blessed be God in his angels and in his saints.

(Traditional)

May the heart of Jesus,
in the Most Blessed Sacrament,
be praised, adored, and loved
with grateful affection,
at every moment,
in all the tabernacles of the world,
even to the end of time. Amen.   (Traditional)

O God, let me rise to the edges of time
and open my life to your eternity;
let me run to the edges of space
and gaze into your immensity;
let me climb through the barriers of sound
and pass into your silence;
and then, in stillness and silence
let me adore You,
who are Life – Light – Love
without beginning and without end,
the Source – the Sustainer –
The Restorer – the Purifier –
of all that is;
the Lover who has bound earth to heaven
by the beams of a cross;
the Healer who has renewed a dying race
by the blood of a chalice;
the God who has taken man into your glory
by the wounds of sacrifice;
God . . . God . . . God . . .
Blessed be God.
Let me adore you.   (Sister Ruth SLG)

O Father of Mercies,
behold this Living Victim
which here and everywhere

your Holy Church offers unto you:
Look upon the Face of your beloved Son,
and accept his Sacrifice for our sins
and for those of the whole world.
>   (From the *Centenary Prayer Book*)*

O God, of your goodness,
give me yourself,
for you are enough for me.
>   (Lady Julian of Norwich, *c.* 1342–*c.* 1416)

The offered Christ is distributed among us. Alleluia!
He gives his body as food,
and his blood he pours out for us. Alleluia!
Draw near to the Lord
and be filled with his light. Alleluia!
Taste and see how sweet is the Lord. Alleluia!
Bless the Lord of Heaven. Alleluia!
Bless him in the highest Heavens. Alleluia!
Bless him all your angels,
bless him all you powers. Alleluia!
>   (Armenian Liturgy)*

O merciful God,
enlighten our hearts with the grace of your Holy
>   Spirit,
that we may worthily receive your holy Sacrament,
and love you with an everlasting love.
May God the Father, God the Son,
and God the Holy Spirit
bless us and be with us all, now and ever.
>   (Percy Dearmer, 1867–1936)*

May the power of your love, Lord Christ,
fiery and sweet,
so absorb our hearts
as to withdraw them from all that is under heaven;

grant that we may be ready
to die for love of your love,
as you died for love of our love. Amen.
(St Francis of Assisi, 1182–1226)

Glory be to God in the highest,
the Creator and Lord of heaven and earth,
the Preserver of all things,
the Father of mercies,
who so loved mankind
as to send his only begotten Son into the world,
to redeem us from sin and misery,
and to obtain for us everlasting life.
Accept, O gracious God,
our praises and thanksgivings
for your infinite mercies towards us.
And teach us, O Lord,
to love you more and serve you better;
through Jesus Christ our Lord. Amen.
(From the Melkite Greek Catholic Liturgy)

If you cannot attend the Eucharist today

O most loving Saviour,
since I cannot have the happiness
of receiving you this day,
suffer me to gather up the precious crumbs
that fall from your table,
and to unite myself to your divine heart
by faith, hope and charity.
I confess that I do not deserve the children's bread
but I venture humbly to declare that
away from you my soul is dried up for thirst
and my heart cast down with faintness.
Come, then, unto me,
O my divine Jesus,
come into my mind to illuminate it with your light;

come into my heart
to enkindle in it the fire of your love,
and to unite it so intimately with your own
that it may be no more I that live
but you that live in me,
and reign in me for ever. Amen.

(Francis Nepveu, 1639–1708,
trans. Francis A. Ryan)*

Spiritual communion

My Jesus, I believe that you are present
in the Blessed Sacrament,
I love you above all things
and I desire you in my soul.
Since I cannot receive you now sacramentally,
come at least spiritually into my soul.
As though you were already
there I embrace you
and unite myself wholly to you;
permit not that I should ever
be separated from you. Amen.

(St Alphonsus Liguori, 1696–1787,
trans. Eugene Grimm, 1835–91)

Prayers after communion from Common Worship

God our creator,
by your gift
the tree of life was set at the heart of the earthly paradise,
and the bread of life at the heart of your Church:
may we who have been nourished at your table on earth
be transformed by the glory of the Saviour's cross
and enjoy the delights of eternity;
through Jesus Christ our Lord.

(Second Sunday before Lent)

Loving God,
as a mother feeds her children at the breast
you feed us in this sacrament with the food and
    drink of eternal life:
help us who have tasted your goodness
to grow in grace within the household of faith;
through Jesus Christ our Lord.   (Mothering Sunday)

Strengthen for service, Lord,
the hands that have taken holy things;
may the ears which have heard your word
    be deaf to clamour and dispute;
may the tongues which have sung your praise
    be free from deceit;
may the eyes which have seen the tokens of your love
    shine with the light of hope;
and may the bodies which have been fed with your body
    be refreshed with the fullness of your life;
glory to you for ever.   (Eighth Sunday after Trinity)

11

Blessing and the world; work and the day's ending

———•·•·•———

Leaving well is as important as arriving well. After having made our communion we are then ready to travel 'in the strength of that food' (1 Kings 19.8) and to take our place in God's mission to the world. Communion can seem very close to the end of the Eucharist – we have hardly got back to our seat than the service is over and we are being dismissed. It is important that this is so. We should be eager to leave the church as much as we are eager to arrive. We have a gospel to proclaim, good news, a word for the world that burns within us and that we are desperate to share.

The disciples wanted to stay on the Mount of the Transfiguration; they declared to Jesus that it was 'good to be here'. We might want to do the same, to stay in the place of divine encounter, to stay in the place of community, to stay in the place of peace. But in baptism we are remade for mission; mission is our gospel imperative, our vocation, and we cannot stay within the walls of the church.

This chapter contains prayers to help us as we leave church and also material that will direct us as we consider our vocation. God has a task for each one of us. Before we were born he knew us and there is a particular task that only we can do for him. Discerning what that vocation might be can be a lengthy task or the realization of a moment, a Damascus-road experience. But we will never know what it is that God is calling us to if we are not expectant and not listening.

The Mass is ended but the daily miracle of God's love will happen again and again, just as, while each day draws to its close, we know that another day of blessing awaits us. In God every ending is but the dawn of a new beginning, for he created the sun and the moon, and in him all things are good.

Prayers of blessing

May the road rise up to meet you.
May the wind be always at your back.
May the sun shine warm upon your face;
the rains fall soft upon your fields
and until we meet again,
may God hold you in the palm of his hand.
(Traditional Gaelic Blessing)

May the Lord bless our going out and our coming in, from this time forth and for evermore. Amen.
(Based on Psalm 121)

The Lord bless us, and preserve us from all evil,
and keep us in eternal life. Amen.
(*Common Worship: Daily Prayer*)

The Aaronic blessing

The Lord bless you and watch over you,
the Lord make his face shine upon you
and be gracious to you,
the Lord look kindly on you
and give you peace. Amen.
(Numbers 6.24–26 as given in *Common Worship*)

May God the Father bless us;
may Christ take care of us;
the Holy Spirit enlighten us all the days of our life.
The Lord be our defender and keeper of body and
    soul, both now and for ever. Amen.
        (Aethelwald, d. 830, Saxon Bishop of Lichfield)

The work of blessing

Christians bless people, places and things. They also
'bless' God, which may seem a very strange thing to
do. After all, blessing makes things holy and God is
already perfectly holy. It becomes clearer when we
see that 'blessed' also means 'happy'. Think of the
Beatitudes, taught by Jesus in Matthew's Gospel:
'Blessed are the poor in spirit . . .' It would not be so
bad to translate these with the word 'happy' – 'Happy
are the poor in spirit . . .' – or with 'perfectly content'
or 'blissfully complete'. When we 'bless God', we talk
about him in this way. 'Blessed be God,' we say at
Benediction. We make it clear that God is happy,
secure, content, complete. It is also a prayer asking
that God be properly acknowledged and praised – like
'Hallowed be thy name' in the Lord's Prayer.

Praise is never far from Christian blessing. Acts
of blessing help us to see things as they are, as gifts
from God, as parts of his good creation. We recognize
this gift and this goodness; we recognize that they
come from God, the Creator of all things and the
giver of all gifts. A blessing thanks him for his gift
and praises him for his goodness.

We also bless things because we realize that the
goodness of the world can be corrupted. Blessings
reclaim things, people and places from evil. This is

one reason why it is good to have your home blessed, perhaps when you first move in. Blessing is also about dedicating things to God's service, such as objects used in worship.

Although we think of blessings as something to do with the authority of a priest, there are some things that only a bishop should bless, such as a new church building, and many things that lay people can bless too. We can all say grace at a meal, which is a kind of blessing, and by ancient custom parents can bless their children.

Blessings are a wonderful part of our tradition and worth getting to know.

Sent out for mission

God of all the nations of the earth,
remember the multitudes who,
though created in your image,
have not known you,
nor the dying of your Son
their Saviour Jesus Christ.
Grant that by the prayers
    and work of your holy Church
they may be delivered from all ignorance and unbelief
and brought to worship you;
through him whom you have sent
to be the resurrection and the life of all people,
your Son Jesus Christ our Lord.

(St Francis Xavier, 1506–52)

Risen Saviour,
you first appeared to Mary Magdalene,
the apostle to the apostles:
Help us hear you when you call our names,

that we, too, may proclaim
the good news of your resurrection
throughout the world,
to the honour and glory of your name. Amen.
(Elizabeth Rankin Geitz)

Lord of light – shine on us;
Lord of peace – dwell in us;
Lord of might – succour us;
Lord of love – enfold us;
Lord of wisdom – enlighten us.
Then, Lord, let us go out as your witnesses,
in obedience to your command;
to share the good news of your mighty love for us
in the gift of your Son,
our Saviour Jesus Christ.   (The Church in Wales)

O Christ our Saviour,
So dwell within us,
that we may go forth
with the light of hope in our eyes,
and the fire of inspiration on our lips,
thy Word on our tongue,
and thy love in our hearts.   (Anonymous)

Prayers of vocation

Gracious God,
you have called me to life
and gifted me in many ways.
Through Baptism you have sent me
to continue the mission of Jesus
by sharing my love with others.
Strengthen me to respond to
your call each day.
Help me to become all you desire of me.
Inspire me to make a difference in others' lives.

Lead me to choose the way of life
you have planned for me.
Open the hearts of all to listen to your call.
Fill all with your Holy Spirit that
we may have listening hearts and
the courage to respond to you.
Enkindle in my heart
and the hearts of others the desire
to make the world a better place. Amen.
(United States Conference of Catholic Bishops)

Prayer for priests

Lord Jesus,
the ministry of priests is a sign of your unfailing
care.
Call from among us the priests needed
for the Church of today and tomorrow.
Bless all students for the priesthood.
Grant them joy, wisdom, courage
and a generous spirit.
Sustain priests with a real sense of your love
and the support of those they are called to serve.
Keep them faithful to their calling. Amen.
(Roman Catholic National Office
for Vocation)

As you leave the church

Now we leave your altar, Lord,
where your Son we have adored,
let our thanks again arise
for this holy sacrifice.
And if thoughts have entered in
which have mixed my prayer with sin,
let your Son's pure blood and grace
all my sinfulness efface.
Sweet it is to worship here,
soon may that bright day appear

when your glory we shall see
and unhindered worship thee. Amen.
>(Taught to AN as a child by the Head Server,
>Bob Hawkins, at All Saints, Wigston Magna)

Prayers as you light a candle

Lord, I'm lighting this candle
because it will burn for longer
than I can pray.   (AN)

Light of the world,
Lord Jesus Christ
accept this light
and the prayer I offer
in your holy name. Amen.   (AN)

Prayers of reflection upon the past day

Prayer at the end of the day

Blessed are you,
O Lord, the God of our fathers,
creator of the changes of day and night,
giving rest to the weary,
renewing the strength of those who are spent,
bestowing upon us occasions of song in the evening.
As you have protected us in the day that is past,
so be with us in the coming night;
keep us from every sin, every evil and every fear;
for you are our light and salvation,
and the strength of our life.
To you be glory for endless ages. Amen.
>(Lancelot Andrewes, 1555–1626)

Gracious God,
you have given us much today;
grant us also a thankful spirit.

Into your hands we commend ourselves
and those we love.
Stay with us,
and when we take our rest
renew us for the service
of your Son Jesus Christ. Amen.

(New Patterns for Worship)

O Lord, support us all the day long
of this troublous life,
until the shades lengthen
and the evening comes,
and the busy world is hushed,
the fever of life is over,
and our work is done.
Then, Lord, in thy mercy,
grant us safe lodging,
a holy rest,
and peace at the last;
through Jesus Christ our Lord.

(John Henry Newman, 1801–90)

Be present, O merciful God,
and protect us through the silent hours of this night,
so that we who are wearied
by the changes and chances of this fleeting world,
may rest upon your eternal changelessness;
through Jesus Christ our Lord.

(From Night Prayer
in *Celebrating Common Prayer*)

Keep watch, dear Lord,
with those who wake, or watch, or weep this night,
and give your angels charge over those who sleep.
Tend the sick,
give rest to the weary,
sustain the dying,

calm the suffering,
and pity the distressed;
all for your love's sake, O Christ our Redeemer.

(after St Augustine of Hippo, 354–430,
Common Worship: Compline)

You know, O God my Father,
what troubles me now,
on recollection,
as I come to my rest.
I seek your forgiveness.
Without your forgiving, sustaining, renewing love
I cannot fully rest.
I commit myself to you anew –
in the name of Jesus my Master. Amen.

(Rita Snowden, 1907–99)

Be the peace of the Spirit
mine this night.
Be the peace of the Son
mine this night.
Be the peace of the Father
mine this night.
The peace of all peace
be mine this night
in the name of the Father,
and of the Son,
and of the Holy Spirit.
Amen.   (Northumbria Community Trust)

Give us light in the night season, we beseech thee, O Lord,
and grant that our rest may be without sin, and our
waking to thy service; that we may come in peace and
safety to the waking of the great day; through Jesus Christ
our Lord. Amen.

A Book of Offices (1914–17),
Episcopal Church in the USA

God be in my head,
and in my understanding;
God be in my eyes,
and in my looking;
God be in my mouth,
and in my speaking;
God be in my heart,
and in my thinking;
God be at my end,
and at my departing.   (Bishop T. B. Strong)

Visit this place, O Lord, we pray,
and drive far from it all the snares of the enemy;
may your holy angels dwell with us
    and guard us in peace,
and may your blessing be always upon us;
through Jesus Christ our Lord. Amen.
    (From Night Prayer, in *Celebrating Common Prayer*)

Appendix
Prayers and devotions

There is such a wealth of material in the catholic tradition that can enhance and enrich our spiritual life. In this section of the book are included forms of prayer and ways of praying that you might find helpful in your own pattern of prayer.

The Rosary

The Rosary is a form of prayer that involves body, voice and mind and is based on the repetition of familiar prayers in a mantra style combined with meditation on mysteries of the faith. The Rosary can be said as a form of intercession. The origin of this form of devotion is traditionally associated with St Dominic (*c.* 1170–1221) and certainly the Dominicans have done a great deal to promote its use. However, the real origins of the Rosary are much more obscure. Some suggest that it grew out of forms of 'people's Psalters' – the repetition of the Our Father and the Hail Mary – which were seen in the medieval era as ways for illiterate laity or travellers who were cut off from the Divine Office to continue to say their prayers. The practice, however, was widely adopted and in 1440 the statutes of Eton College required the pupils to recite daily 'the complete psalter of the Blessed Virgin, consisting of *Credo*, 15 *Paters*, and 150 *Ave Marias*'. The use of the Rosary developed across Europe in the fifteenth century and it continues to be encouraged as a scriptural form of prayer which is accessible to all.

The Rosary begins with the Apostles' Creed:
I believe in God the Father almighty,
Creator of heaven and earth:
and in Jesus Christ his only Son our Lord,
who was conceived by the Holy Spirit,
born of the Virgin Mary,
suffered under Pontius Pilate,
was crucified, died, and was buried.
He descended into hell;
the third day he rose again from the dead;
he ascended into heaven,
he is seated at the right hand of God the Father almighty;
from thence he shall come to judge the living and the
    dead.
I believe in the Holy Spirit;
the holy catholic Church;
the communion of saints;
the forgiveness of sins;
the resurrection of the body,
and the life everlasting.
Amen.

We say the Our Father:
Our Father, who art in heaven,
hallowed be thy name;
Thy kingdom come,
Thy will be done,
on earth as it is in heaven.
Give us this day our daily bread,
and forgive us our trespasses,
as we forgive those who trespass against us;
and lead us not into temptation;
but deliver us from evil.
Amen.

We then say the Hail Mary three times:
Hail Mary, full of grace, the Lord is with thee.
Blessed art thou among women and blessed is the
fruit of thy womb, Jesus.
Holy Mary, Mother of God, pray for us sinners,
now, and at the hour of our death. Amen.

We conclude with the Gloria:
Glory be to the Father, and to the Son and to
the Holy Spirit;
as it was in the beginning, is now and ever
shall be,
world without end. Amen.

The five decades of one of the series of Mysteries
then begin. The Mysteries of the Rosary are a series of
events in the life of Jesus and Mary, which are defined
in four ways – the Joyful Mysteries, which are the events
surrounding the nativity, the Luminous Mysteries,
which focus on the ministry of Jesus, the Sorrowful
Mysteries, which surround his passion and death, and the
Glorious Mysteries, which celebrate his resurrection and
glorification.

For each decade the pattern is the same:

We meditate on the mystery.
We offer intercession.
We say the Our Father.
We say ten Hail Marys.
We conclude with the Gloria.

The Joyful Mysteries
1 The Annunciation of the Lord
2 The Visitation of Our Lady to her cousin Elizabeth
3 The Nativity of the Lord

4 The Presentation of Christ in the Temple
5 The Finding of the Lord in the Temple by his anxious
   parents

The Luminous Mysteries

1 The Baptism in the Jordan
2 The Wedding at Cana
3 The Proclamation of the Kingdom
4 The Transfiguration
5 The Institution of the Eucharist

The Sorrowful Mysteries

1 The Agony in the garden
2 The Scourging at the pillar
3 The Crowning with thorns
4 The Carrying of his cross
5 The Crucifixion

The Glorious Mysteries

1 The Resurrection
2 The Ascension
3 The Descent of the Holy Spirit
4 The Assumption of Mary
5 The Coronation of the Blessed Virgin Mary

*After the five decades are complete, the following anthem to
Our Lady and Collect are said:*
   Hail, Holy Queen, Mother of Mercy!
   Hail, our life, our sweetness and our hope.
   To thee do we cry, poor banished children of Eve;
   to thee do we send up our sighs,
   mourning and weeping in this vale of tears.
   Turn, then, most gracious advocate,
   thine eyes of mercy towards us;
   and after this our exile,

show unto us the blessed fruit of thy womb, Jesus.
O clement, O loving, O sweet Virgin Mary.

Pray for us, Holy Mother of God.
That we may be made worthy of the promises of
    Christ.

Let us pray.
O God, whose only Son, by his life, death and resurrection,
has purchased for us the rewards of eternal life; grant, we
beseech you, that, meditating upon these mysteries of the
Most Holy Rosary of the Blessed Virgin Mary, we may
imitate what they contain and obtain what they promise,
through the same Christ our Lord. Amen.

Praying with objects

We live in a world full of human beings. It is also
a world full of the objects that human beings make
and use. Making and using are vital parts of who we
are.

Human objects are everywhere, so it is not surpris-
ing that they play a part in the definitive human
activity which is prayer. We use prayer cards and
prayer books – like this one – to put the Christian
tradition of prayers into our hands. The lists and
calendars we use to organize our prayers are objects
too. They give us a cycle of people and concerns,
dividing them up across the days of the week and
month.

There are some repetitive forms of prayer that call
for us to keep track of prayers moment by moment.
For the Jesus Prayer of the Orthodox Churches there
are ropes with knots; for the Rosary there are strings
of beads.

There are also objects to provide us with things to think about as we pray. With an icon, picture or crucifix we can meditate upon some central event from the history of redemption. With a Bible to hand, we might base our prayer around a sentence or story, or we might let our prayers jump off from a short reading from the tradition of the Church, perhaps from one of the early Fathers.

Making your confession

While many people nowadays see nothing wrong with having a therapist or a counsellor with whom to talk things through, the idea of making a sacramental confession seems to be a step too far. Not that therapy and the confessional are the same except that in both situations, in a confidential environment and with another person, we are able to open up our lives and our self and reflect on where we are.

The term 'sacramental confession' refers to the one-to-one occasion with a priest in which a confession is heard, and advice and penance are given before absolution is pronounced. It stands alongside and complements our usual experience of confession in the liturgy. The kind of confession in that context we call 'general confession'. The sins which we confess are formal and general rather than specific and so the absolution is similarly general.

It is a popular misunderstanding of the Anglican tradition that sacramental confession disappeared at the Reformation. This ignores the fact that the authors of the Book of Common Prayer included it in 'The Visitation of the Sick', though it was envisaged that this was for those who were 'very sick' rather than as a regular part of someone's devotional life.

It was in a Scottish proverb that it was said that 'confession is good for the soul'. It is good for those who are seeking to draw closer to God by taking their own relationship with God seriously. The Anglican guidance with regard to sacramental confession that 'all may, some should, none must' remains true. But that means that we should all consider whether we should.

Preparing for a first confession

The greatest hurdle in making a first confession, especially if we are an adult, is not so much in making the confession but deciding what we should confess. With a lifetime of sin behind us what should we choose to say?

When preparing to make a first confession it is good to be able to prepare beforehand by sitting down with a priest, with your spiritual director or 'soul friend' and talking through what you will be doing. That conversation may not be about specifics but about confession more generally and what we mean by sin. In the light of that conversation it may well be easier to decide what it is that you should be confessing.

Preparing for any confession

It is important to give time to preparing your confession before you go to make it. In many ways the preparation is almost as important as hearing the words of the absolution. Oscar Wilde wrote that 'It is the confession, not the priest, that gives us absolution' (*The Picture of Dorian Gray*). In this he is partly right: there is something very important about the actual process of remembering those things that have separated you from God, from your neighbour and from yourself – the things that we call sin. Remembering them and repenting of them have to come before absolution.

A checklist of sins can never be exhaustive but can suggest areas we should consider when preparing to make a confession. Remember that sins can be of two kinds: sins of commission, the things you did that you should not have done, and sins of omission, the things you did not do that you should have done. And what can appear as a good thing can have a reverse and darker side, so that a virtue can become a vice.

The following form of prayer is taken from *Common Worship*, into which have been set some suggestions of what you might think about when preparing your confession. The prayer is followed by an act of contrition that you might say.

Almighty God,
long-suffering and of great goodness:
I confess to you,
I confess with my whole heart
my neglect and forgetfulness of your commandments,
my wrong doing, thinking, and speaking;
the hurts I have done to others,
and the good I have left undone.
In particular I confess
[since my last confession in . . . /
in this my first confession . . .]

Against God

not going to church; not making your communion; not reading the Bible; not saying your prayers; blaspheming God's name; ignoring God's call; refusing God's will; not committing yourself to stewardship of money and time.

Against your neighbour

anger; jealousy; acts of violence or abuse; unfaithfulness; prejudice; disregard for the environment; exploitation of other living beings.

Against yourself

gluttony; addiction; pride; self-loathing; laziness; not using your talents; living beyond your means.

> O God, for these, and all other sins that I cannot
>   now remember,
> I ask your forgiveness.
> Forgive me, for I have sinned against you;
> and raise me to newness of life;
> through Jesus Christ our Lord. Amen.

> My God, for love of you
> I desire to hate and forsake all sins
> by which I have ever displeased you;
> and I resolve by the help of your grace
> to commit them no more;
> and to avoid all opportunities of sin.
> Help me to do this,
> through Jesus Christ our Lord. Amen.

Following your confession

After you have made your confession and before the priest pronounces absolution there will be an opportunity to talk about anything that you have mentioned and the priest will then suggest a 'penance'. God's forgiveness is freely given and the penance is not a payment that you are making for what was won for you on the cross, but a way for you to continue your meditation on the love of God for you. The priest may suggest a prayer for you to say, a passage from Scripture or a psalm for you to read, or an action you might perform.

And before you leave the church give thanks to God for the generous love that you have experienced.

> Loving God,
> as the woman who anointed your son
> loved much for much had been forgiven her,

so I offer my love and my life to you
for you have forgiven me so much this day,
and in the strength of your grace
I seek to follow you more closely
from this day and for evermore. Amen.   (AN)

An examination of conscience

O Holy God, enlighten my mind with the light of thy truth
that I may know myself as I am and may discover all my
sins and shortcomings; and give me grace to confess them
with true sorrow of heart and firm purpose of amendment
of life. Amen.

Then spend some time considering your life since you last
made a confession or recollected your sins. Reminding
yourself of the Summary of the Law will help you do
this.

Our Lord Jesus Christ said:
The first commandment is this:
'Hear, O Israel, the Lord our God is the only Lord.
You shall love the Lord your God
   with all your heart,
with all your soul, with all your mind,
and with all your strength.'
The second is this: 'Love your neighbour as yourself.'
There is no other commandment greater than these.
On these two commandments hang
   all the law and the prophets.

A rule of life

It is good practice to establish for yourself a simple rule
of life by which you will live. This does not need to be
complex and it should be achievable. In setting the rule

for his monastic communities St Benedict wrote this in the Prologue to his Rule:

> In drawing up its regulations we hope to set down nothing harsh, nothing burdensome ... Do not be daunted immediately by fear and run away from the road that leads to salvation. It is bound to be narrow at the outset. But as we progress in the way of life and in faith, we shall run on the path of God's commandments, our hearts overflowing with the inexpressible delight of love.
>
> (Rule of St Benedict, trans. Joan Chittister)

These are the areas you should consider. Pray about each one and ask God to help you keep the rule that you decide will help you in living out your Christian faith. Reflecting on your rule of life and how you have kept it will enable you to prepare for your confession.

1. The Eucharist – how often will I attend the Eucharist and receive communion? Every Sunday? During the week? Daily?
2. Prayer – when and how often am I going to pray? In the morning? In the evening? Before I go to sleep?
3. Bible reading – when and how will I read the Bible? Each day? Using notes as a guide? With friends in a group?
4. Giving – how much can I commit to giving to others? A tithe? Will I divide this between the church and other charities? When will I review my giving?
5. Confession – will I make a sacramental confession to a priest? Will I talk with someone about my own spiritual journey? How often will I do this?
6. Mission – how will I share the gospel with others?

What task will I commit myself to in the life of my church?

7 Retreat – will I make a retreat each year? Will it be for a day, a weekend or longer?

8 The environment – how will I live as a good steward of all that God has entrusted me with? How can I walk gently on the earth?

9 Family and friends – how much time will I commit to other people? How will I keep in touch with those I seldom see? How will I keep my relationships alive and healthy?

10 Rest – how will I take my rest? How much sleep do I need? How will I treat my body with respect?

How to pray better

1 Make prayer a regular feature of every day – keep the conversation going.

2 Establish a pattern to your spiritual life:
   (a) daily
   (b) weekly
   (c) monthly
   (d) quarterly
   (e) twice yearly
   (f) annually

3 Be realistic.

4 Organize your intercessions – keep a prayer diary.

5 When the well runs dry don't give up.

6 Get a spiritual director.

7 Create a knapsack of prayers.

8 Pray, rather than just reading about prayer.

9 Expose yourself to silence.

10 Accept the fact that God loves you.

Prayers before and after a journey or pilgrimage

The itinerarium

This service is used before pilgrims set out on a journey.

Antiphon: May God, almighty and merciful, lead us by
peaceful and secure paths, and may the angel Raphael be
our companion on the way, that we may return home in
safety and joy.

Blessed be the Lord the God of Israel,
who has come to his people and set them free.
He has raised up for us a mighty Saviour,
born of the house of his servant David.
Through his holy prophets God promised of old
to save us from our enemies,
from the hands of all that hate us,
To show mercy to our ancestors,
and to remember his holy covenant.
This was the oath God swore to our father Abraham:
to set us free from the hands of our enemies,
Free to worship him without fear,
holy and righteous in his sight
all the days of our life.
And you, child, shall be called
    the prophet of the Most High
for you will go before the Lord to prepare his way,
To give his people knowledge of salvation
by the forgiveness of all their sins.
In the tender compassion of our God
the dawn from on high shall break upon us,
To shine on those who dwell in darkness
    and the shadow of death,
and to guide our feet into the way of peace.

Glory to the Father and to the Son
and to the Holy Spirit;
as it was in the beginning is now
and shall be for ever. Amen.

Repeat antiphon.

Lord have mercy upon us. Christ have mercy upon us.
Lord have mercy upon us.

Our Father . . .

O God, save your servants.
Who put their trust in you.

Be to us a tower of strength, O Lord.
Against every enemy.

Show us, O Lord, your ways.
And teach us your paths.

God shall give his angels charge over you.
To keep you in all your ways.

O Lord, hear my prayer.
And let my cry come before you.

O God, you brought the children of Israel through the
sea with dry feet, and the wise men found their way to
you by the guiding of a star: grant us a safe journey and
peaceful days. With your holy Angel as our companion,
may we reach the place to which we travel, and come at
last to the harbour of eternal salvation. Amen.

Lord, watch over us your servants, as you led your servant
Abraham and kept him safe in all his wanderings. Be
to us, Lord, a help in preparation, comfort on the way,
shade in heat, shelter in rain and cold, a carriage in tired-
ness, a shield in adversity, a staff in insecurity, a haven in
accident. Under your guidance, may we reach our destin-
ation in happiness, and finally return safely to our homes.
Amen.

Almighty God, may your family may advance upon the
path of salvation. Following the preaching of John the

Baptist, who prepared the way, may we come in peace to the one he foretold, Jesus Christ, your Son, our Lord, who lives and reigns with you in the unity of the Holy Spirit, One God, for ever and ever. Amen.

Let us go forth in peace.
In the Name ✠ of the Lord. Amen.

Before a journey
This ancient prayer for travellers, the Itinerarium, grew up in the early monasteries. St Benedict urged those early monks to 'commend themselves to the prayers of all the brethren and to the abbot'. The longer a monk's journey, the longer the prayers that were recited. Even if we reserve the full set of prayers given here for our more arduous journeys, or for pilgrimages, it reminds us to make a simple prayer before we leave the house any day. We should also give thanks when the journey is done.

The second collect here describes God with vivid physical images: the shade of a tree, the firmness of a staff, the security of a harbour. In this poetry there is a great insight: God is beyond all created things but is only encountered through them. This might happen through the words of the Bible, the beauty of the view from a train window, or the kindness of a fellow traveller. Whatever goodness or joy we encounter in our journeys comes to us from God. This prayer encourages us to trace them back to him, as much in the ordinary things of life as in the extra-ordinary. If we learn to look at the world in that way as we travel through it, then everything good that crosses our path offers us a glimpse of God's love.

A shorter set of prayers before a journey

In the name of the Father and of the Son and of the Holy Spirit. Amen.

The Lord be with you.
And also with you.

Responsorial Psalm 122
Response: We will go up with joy to the house of our God.

I rejoiced when I heard them say:
Let us go to God's house.
And now our feet are standing:
within your gates O Jerusalem. *R.*
Jerusalem is built as a city: at unity in itself.
It is there that the tribes go up:
the tribes of the Lord. *R.*
O pray for the peace of Jerusalem:
may they prosper that love you;
May peace reign in your walls,
    in your palaces peace. *R.*
For the sake of my kinsfolk and friends,
I will pray that peace be with you;
for the sake of the house of our God,
I will pray for your good. *R.*

Lord God, who called our father Abraham
to journey into the unknown,
and guarded him and blessed him on his way,
protect us too and bless our journey.
May your confidence support us as we set out,
your Spirit be with us on our way,
and lead us back to our homes in peace.
Those we love we commend to your care,
You are with them, we shall not fear.
So, Lord, be our companion on our journey,
and let it draw us closer to you,
as we seek to follow in the steps of your Son,
our Saviour Jesus Christ. Amen.

Mary, Mother of God,
pray for us.
All Saints of God,
pray for us.
Holy angels of God,
watch over us.

May the Lord lead you forth in peace
and grant you your heart's desire:
and the blessing of God Almighty,
the Father, the Son and the Holy Spirit,
be amongst you and remain with you always. Amen.

If this is a pilgrimage, the pilgrims may be sprinkled with holy water by a priest.

Let us go forth in peace.
In the name of Christ. Amen.

Sources and acknowledgements

————•◆•————

The publisher and authors acknowledge with thanks permission to reproduce extracts from copyright material reproduced in this book.

Every effort has been made to seek permission to use copyright material. The publisher apologizes for those cases where permission might not have been sought and, if notified, will formally seek permission at the earliest opportunity.

APD as a source for the prayers in this book means Andrew Davison, AN means Andrew Nunn and TW means Toby Wright. Prayers marked * have been modernized or adapted. Where no translator is given, the translator is either of one of the authors of this volume, or is unknown.

Bible

Scripture quotations are from the New Revised Standard Version of the Bible, Anglicized Edition, copyright © 1989, 1995 by the Division of Christian Education of the National Council of the Churches of Christ in the USA. Used by permission. All rights reserved.

Prayer books

Extracts from *Common Worship: Services and Prayers* are copyright © The Archbishops' Council, 2000, and are reproduced by permission. Extracts from *Common Worship: Additional Collects* are copyright © The Archbishops' Council and are reproduced by permission. Extracts from *Common Worship: Daily Prayer* are copyright ©

The Archbishops' Council, 2005, and are reproduced by permission. Extracts from *Common Worship: Christian Initiation* are copyright © The Archbishops' Council, 2006, and are reproduced by permission. Extracts from *Common Worship: Pastoral Services* are copyright © The Archbishops' Council, 2008, and are reproduced by permission. Extracts from *New Patterns for Worship* are copyright © The Archbishops' Council, 2008, and are reproduced by permission.

Extracts from The Book of Common Prayer, the rights in which are vested in the Crown, are reproduced by permission of the Crown's Patentee, Cambridge University Press.

Material from *Celebrating Common Prayer* (1992) and *Celebrating Common Prayer: The Pocket Version* (1994), ed. David Stancliffe and Brother Tristam ssf, is copyright © the European Province of the Society of St Francis 1992 and 1994.

The translations of the Benedictus and the Te Deum Laudamus are from *Praying Together*, copyright © ELLC (the English Language Liturgical Consultation) 1998.

'A litany of penitence' is copyright to ICEL (the International Commission on English in the Liturgy).

'Blessed Lord, who caused all holy Scriptures' and 'Almighty and everlasting God, you have given us your servants grace' are originally from The Book of Common Prayer and are copyright to Cambridge University Press. See acknowledgement above.

'Almighty and eternal God, you have revealed yourself' is copyright to Oxford University Press.

Other publications

'You are holy, Lord' and 'May the power of your love, Lord Christ' are from *Celebrating Common Prayer*. See acknowledgement above.

'Worthy of praise from every mouth', 'We give you hearty thanks', 'O God, make us children of quietness' and 'O Holy

Spirit, the Comforter' are adapted from the translation given in *A Diary of Prayer*, ed. Elizabeth Goudge (London: Spire, 1966).

'My life is an instant' by St Thérèse of Lisieux (translator unknown), 'O Lord, the Scripture says', 'Lord, how much juice', 'Almighty and everlasting God, who formed your Church' by the Community of the Resurrection, 'We pray you, Lord', 'Most merciful Father' by Michael Ramsey, 'God our deliverer' by David Stancliffe and 'Eternal God, on you have I depended' are from *The SPCK Book of Christian Prayer* (London: SPCK, 1995).

The prayer based on words from the Rule of Taizé is from *Parable of Community: The Rule and Other Basic Texts of Taizé* by Brother Roger (New York: Seabury Press, 1981).

'My Father, I abandon myself to you' by Blessed Charles de Foucauld is from *2000 Years of Prayer* by Michael Counsell (Norwich: Canterbury Press, 1999).

Extracts by James Ferguson are from *Prayers for Common Worship* (London: Allenson and Co., 1937) and are copyright to the Lutterworth Press.

'O God, who hast ordained' is from Samuel Johnson, 'Prayers and meditations', in James Boswell, *Life of Dr Johnson* (1776).

'O Lord Jesus Christ', 'O Lord Jesus Christ, Son of God', 'Pray to God for me' and 'Supreme Leaders of the Heavenly Hosts' are adapted from *A Manual of Eastern Orthodox Prayers* (Crestwood, NY: St Vladimir's Seminary Press, 1994).

'O Lord our God' by St Anselm is amended from a prayer based on a passage in the *Proslogion* and can be found at <www.thisischurch.com>.

'We adore you' by St Francis of Assisi can be found at <www.franciscans.org.uk>.

'Divine Saviour' by St Francis de Sales can be found at <www.catholic.org/prayer/prayer.php?p>.

The belfry prayer is from the Kent County Association of Change Ringers and is reproduced by permission of the Revd Justin Lewis-Anthony.

The altar servers' prayer can be found at <www.import antprayers.com>.

The RSCM Choristers' Prayer was first published by the School of English Church Music in 1934 in the *Choristers' Pocket Book*.

The lectors' prayer can be found at <www.appleseeds. org/lector_prayer.htm>.

The eucharistic ministers' prayer can be found on the website of Sacred Heart Parish, Quincy, USA (<www. sacredheartquincy.org>).

'O God, who by the Baptism', 'Almighty God, we invoke you', 'O God the Father, good beyond all that is good' and 'O God, the Life of the faithful' are from William Bright, *Ancient Collects and Other Prayers Selected from Various Rituals* (Oxford: Parker, 1864).

'God and Father of us all' and 'Almighty God, we rejoice to know' are from Frank Colquhoun, *New Parish Prayers* (London: Hodder & Stoughton, 2005).

'Almighty God, long-suffering and of great goodness' is adapted from Eric Milner-White, *My God, My Glory* (London: SPCK, 1967).

'Lord, by this sweet and saving Sign' is from Eric Milner-White, *Procession of Passion Prayers* (London: SPCK, 1932). The first two lines are by Richard Crashaw (1612–49).

'Lord, I will strive earnestly' and 'O merciful God, enlighten our hearts' are from Percy Dearmer, *The Sanctuary: A Book for Communicants* (London: Rivingtons, 1958).

'O Lord, remember not only' (prayer written by an unknown prisoner in Ravensbruck concentration camp) is from Mary Craig, *Blessings* (London: Hodder & Stoughton, 1997).

'Merciful Lord, with a pure heart' and 'Almighty God, give us wisdom to perceive you' are from Ampleforth Abbey, *St Benedict's Prayer Book* (Leominster: Gracewing, 1994).

'In silence to be there before you' is from Michel Quoist, *Prayers of Life*, trans. A. M. de Commaile and A. M. Forsyth (Dublin: Gill and Macmillan, 1965).

'O God, whose beauty is beyond our imagining' is slightly adapted from Janet Morley, *All Desires Known* (London: SPCK, 2005). It is copyright to SPCK.

'O God, whose love is without measure' by Br Ramon SSF is from Joyce Huggett and Brother Ramon, *Heaven on Earth: Personal Retreat Programme* (London: HarperCollins, 1991).

'Lord, as I read the psalms' by St Gregory of Nazianzus is from *Early Christian Prayers*, ed. A. Hamman (London: Longmans, Green & Co.; Chicago, IL: Regnary, 1961).

'Almighty God, who hast taught us' is from Rowland Williams, *Psalms and Litanies* (London: Williams and Northgate, 1876).

'O Christ, my Lord' is from George Appleton, *One Man's Prayers* (London: SPCK, 1967).

'My Lord God, I have no idea where I am going' by Thomas Merton is from his *Dialogues with Silence* (San Francisco, CA: HarperSanFrancisco, 2001; London: SPCK, 2002).

'O Holy Spirit, giver of light and life' is from Eric Milner-White and G. W. Briggs, *Daily Prayer* (London: SPCK, 1941).

'O God, who spread your creating arms' is adapted from F. E. Brightman, *Eastern Liturgies* (Oxford: Clarendon Press, 1896; repr. Piscataway, NJ: Gorgias Press, 2004).

'Almighty and everlasting God, who formed your Church' is copyright to the Community of the Resurrection.

'Creator God, you made all things', 'God our Father, you are present to your people everywhere' and 'God of all grace and comfort' are from the Church of Scotland's *Book of Common Order* (Edinburgh: Saint Andrew Press, 1994).

'God of justice', 'As I enter the street market' and 'Creator God, you loved the world into life' are copyright © Christian Aid.

'O God the Father of all' by Blessed Teresa of Calcutta is from Kathryn Spink, *Mother Teresa: A Complete Authorized Biography* (San Francisco, CA: HarperSanFrancisco, 1998).

'Almighty God, who alone can guard' is from Richard Littledale and Edward Vaux, *The Priest's Prayer Book* (London: Joseph Masters, 1870).

'Almighty and everlasting God, grant to this home' and 'We thank you, most gracious God' are from *The Book of Occasional Services* © 2004 by the Church Pension Fund. All rights reserved. Used by permission of Church Publishing Incorporated, New York, NY.

'Into your strong hands, our Father', 'May the God of all love' and 'Almighty God, we rejoice to know' are from *New Parish Prayers*, ed. Frank Colquhoun (London: Hodder & Stoughton, 2005).

'Merciful Saviour' and 'O Lord our heavenly Father' are excerpted from the *Book of Common Prayer*, © 1962 by the General Synod of The Anglican Church of Canada. Used with permission.

'Our Master, Jesus Christ', 'Almighty and everlasting God, who dost enkindle' and 'May God the Father bless us' are from Selina Fitzherbert Fox, *A Chain of Prayer Across the Ages: Forty Centuries of Prayer, 2000 BC–AD 1923* (New York: E. P. Dutton, 1928).

'O Lord Jesus Christ, Son of the living God' and 'Almighty God, the fountain of all wisdom' are from the *Book of Common Prayer* of the Episcopal Church in the USA (1979).

'Upon the heavenly altar' is from *Liturgies and Other Divine Offices of the Church* (London: G. Barclay, 1853).

'O Almighty God, the Father of all humanity' can be found on the website of the Christian Classics Ethereal Library (<www.ccel.org/node/4524>).

'O God, who would fold' is from Eric Milner-White, *Memorials upon Several Occasions* (London: A. R. Mowbray, 1933).

'O Christ, the peace of the things that are on high', 'O God, the unsearchable abyss of peace', 'O Master, our Lord and our God' and 'The offered Christ is distributed among us' are from *Eucharistic Prayers from the Ancient Liturgies*, ed. Evelyn Underhill (London and New York: Longmans, Green and Co., 1939).

'Christ our Hope' is from *The Lion Prayer Collection* (Oxford: Lion Hudson, 1992).

'Into his joy, the Lord has received you' is by the Benedictine Community at St Mary's Abbey, West Malling, Kent ME19 6JX. The words were composed by a Malling Abbey nun, then set to music composed by another nun of the community.

Ave, Regina caelorum is translated by the Benedictine Community at Stanbrook Abbey, Wass, Yorkshire YO61 4AY.

Salve Regina is from *The Divine Office* (London: Collins, 2006).

'Lord Jesus Christ, by taking human flesh' is adapted from a prayer from the Church of England Central Board of Finance, copyright to the Archbishops' Council of the Church of England.

'Generous God, you are Life' is adapted by the General Synod of the Scottish Episcopal Church.

'For food in a world where many walk in hunger' can be found on the website of the Huron Hunger Fund (<www.diohuron.org/parishes_ministries/HHF/huronhungerfund.htm>).

'The eyes of all wait upon you, O God' and 'Bless the Lord, O my soul' are from the Society of St Francis,

Celebrating Common Prayer: The Pocket Version, 2nd edn (London: Continuum, 2002).

'Come, true light' is translated by Kallistos Ware in *The Orthodox Way* (Crestwood, NY: St Vladimir's Seminary Press, 1995).

'God, lover of us all' is from the St Hilda Community, *The New Women Included* (London: SPCK, 1996). Copyright for this prayer is held by Lala Winkley.

'We give thanks to you, our Father' (the *Didache*) is translated by R. C. D. Jasper and G. J. Cuming in *Prayers of the Eucharist: Early and Reformed*, 3rd edn. Copyright 1990. Published by Liturgical Press, Collegeville, Minnesota. Reprinted with permission.

'Let us make our way together' by St Teresa of Avila is from *Praying with Saint Teresa*, ed. Paula Clifford (London: SPCK, 1988).

'My spirit has become dry' from *Sayings of Light and Love* by St John of the Cross is from *The Complete Works of St John of the Cross*, trans. E. Allison Peers (London: Burns and Oates, 1933).

'From thee we came' is from John Hunter, *Devotional Services for Public Worship*, 6th edn (Glasgow: James Maclehose, 1895; repr. Whitefish, MT: Kessinger, 2008).

'O God, let me rise to the edges of time', copyright to the Sisters of the Love of God at the Convent of the Incarnation, Fairacres, Oxford, is from *The Oxford Book of Prayer*, ed. George Appleton (Oxford: Oxford University Press, 2002).

'O Father of Mercies' is adapted from the *Centenary Prayer Book* (London: Church Literature Association, 1933).

'O God, of your goodness' by Julian of Norwich is from *Revelations of Divine Love*, ed. Roger Hudleston (London: Burns & Oates, 1927).

'Risen Saviour' by Elizabeth Rankin Geitz is from *Women's Uncommon Prayers*, ed. E. R. Geitz, K. McCormick and T. J. Sukraw (Harrisburg, PA: Morehouse Publishing, 2000).

'Gracious God, you have called me to life' can be found on the website of the US Conference of Catholic Bishops (<www.usccb.org/vocations/prayereng.shtml>).

'Lord Jesus, the ministry of priests is a sign' can be found on the website of the Roman Catholic National Office for Vocation (<www.ukvocation.org/prayers/voc_pray.html>), an office of the Bishops' Conference for England and Wales.

'O Lord, support us all the day long' is from John Henry Newman, Sermon 20 in *Sermons on Subjects of the Day* (London: J. G. F. and J. Rivington; Oxford: J. H. Parker, 1843).

'You know, O God my Father' by Rita Snowden is from *Prayers for Busy People* (London: HarperCollins, 1978).

'Be the peace of the Spirit' is copyright © The Northumbria Community Trust, Nether Springs, Chatton, Northumberland NE66 5SD.

The extract from the Rule of St Benedict is translated in Joan Chittister OSB, *The Rule of Benedict: Insights for the Ages* (New York: Crossroad; Middlegreen, Slough: St Pauls, 1992).

Suggestions for further reading

There are so many prayer books available that it can seem confusing to those looking for guidance and help in their prayer life. Any visit to a good Christian bookshop will provide a lot of inspiration to encourage different ways and styles of praying. If you have heard of Celtic prayer for instance and would like to learn more about it, there is a wealth of material written and collected by David Adam, the Iona Community and people such as Kathy Galloway. What is true for Celtic prayer is true for all traditions of spirituality within the Church and you are encouraged to have a go and discover the riches of the tradition in which we share.

For those wishing to pray in a more structured way each day, the revision of the daily office in the Church of England has produced a wonderfully rich pattern of prayer which is adaptable to all circumstances.

Common Worship: Daily Prayer (Church House Publishing) provides the full text and all the options. You have to have a copy of the lectionary and a Bible with it in order to say Morning and Evening Prayer, but it is well worth persevering with as it can be enormously enriching.

A very user-friendly version of *Daily Prayer* which requires no lectionary or Bible but can be carried with you wherever you go is *Celebrating Daily Prayer: A Version of Common Worship Daily Prayer* (Morehouse). This is an invaluable version of the main book, and one which contains a wealth of other prayer resources.

Another edition which is also very usable is called *Time to Pray* (Church House Publishing). It contains Prayer During the Day and Night Prayer from *Common Worship* with selected psalms and prayers and is both easily portable and accessible.

Much of the recent revision of the daily office has been resourced by the Anglican Franciscans (the Society of St Francis ssf) who produced the enormously popular *Celebrating Common Prayer*. This is available in many versions including pocket-sized editions.

Praying is always an adventure in encountering God, and so moving on to the next step of the journey and the adventure is something that every Christian should do.

Some further suggestions

Anthony Bloom, *Living Prayer* (London: Libra, 1966)

Stephen Cottrell, *Praying Through Life* (London: Church House Publishing, 2003)

Richard Harries, *Prayer and the Pursuit of Happiness* (London: Fount, 1985)

Christopher Jamison, *Finding Sanctuary* (London: Phoenix Press, 2007)

Kenneth Leech, *True Prayer: An Introduction to Christian Spirituality* (London: Sheldon Press, 1980)

Mother Mary Clare slg, *Encountering the Depths* (Oxford: SLG Press, 1973)

Herbert McCabe op, essays on prayer in *God Matters* and *God Still Matters* (London: Continuum, 2000 and 2002)

Simon Tugwell op, *Prayer: Living with God* and *Prayer in Practice* (Dublin: Veritas, 1974)

Index

PRAYERS

absence from the Eucharist
103
after receiving communion
104
all-purpose prayers 43
angels 86
Angelus 75

baptism 11
beginning of the day 4
beginning intercession 42
beginning of work 6
Bible
  prayers from the Bible 33
  before reading the Bible 31, 36
birthday 56
blessing 107

carers 53
Church 46
collects from the Book of
  Common Prayer 25
collects from *Common
  Worship* 27
confession 121

dead 61
death 60, 94
dedication to God 5

economic crisis 57
end of the day 112
ending intercessions 64
enemies 57
entering a church 7
environment 49
examination of conscience 15,
  125

faith 37
family and friends 54

godparents and godchildren
  12
grace at meals 79
graveside 63

Holy Spirit 87
home 54
honouring the Blessed
  Sacrament 100

justice 51

leaders 48
leaving church 111

marriage 56
Mary, the Blessed Virgin
  73
mission 109

morning 4
mystery of God 30

needy 57, 93
night 112

passing a church 7
peace 50, 69
penitence
    amendment 18
    after confession 19, 124
    making confession 121
    prayers for pardon 16
    preparation 15, 122
praise 2
preparing for ministry 8
preparing for worship 8
priests 11, 111

receiving communion 99
Regina caeli 76
Rosary 116

saints 64, 71
sick 58
silence 23
stewardship 78

thanksgiving 83
travellers and journeys 53, 128

vocation 110

workers 51
world 47

THOUGHTS ON PRAYER

blessing 108
body 21

confession 121

dead 60
does prayer change
    anything? 13

Further reading 142

journeys 130

offering of the Mass
    90

rule of life 125

saints 71
silence 24

Trinity 39

with objects 120
with others 97
without ceasing 81